Casual But Effective Prayers

Alexander Ikomoni
Angela Ikomoni

Father, I thank You that You have heard Me.

JOHN 11:41B

TRILOGY CHRISTIAN PUBLISHERS

Tustin, CA

Trilogy Christian Publishers

A Wholly Owned Subsidiary of Trinity Broadcasting Network

2442 Michelle Drive

Tustin, CA 92780

Casual But Effective Prayers

Rights Department, 2442 Michelle Drive, Tustin, CA 92780.

Trilogy Christian Publishing/TBN and colophon are trademarks of Trinity Broadcasting Network.

Cover design by Jeff Summers

For information about special discounts for bulk purchases, please contact Trilogy Christian Publishing.

Trilogy Disclaimer: The views and content expressed in this book are those of the author and may not necessarily reflect the views and doctrine of Trilogy Christian Publishing or the Trinity Broadcasting Network.

Manufactured in the United States of America

10 9 8 7 6 5 4 3 2 1

Library of Congress Cataloging-in-Publication Data is available.

ISBN: 978-1-68556-931-0

E-ISBN: 978-1-68556-932-7 (ebook)

Casual but Effective Prayers

by

Dr. Alexander Ikomoni

Dr. Angela Ikomoni

Editing by Concierge Librarian

Forewords

by

Ambassador Samson Itegboje

Sharon Osadebamwen

Dr. Olayinka Olubunmi

Dedication

We are grateful for the gift of love and support of our family as we start this project of writing our book. My wife, Dr. Angela, and I dedicate this book to our three children: our daughters, Natassia and Alexandria, and our only begotten son, A. J. Ikomoni. We love the adults and young adults who you have grown up to become. We know that it is only by the grace of God and prayers that you are spiritually rooted.

And we also dedicate this book to our parents, who labored and prayed us through to victory: Esther Oyovikevwe Ikomoni, née Obiku (late), and Chief Godwin Jigidah Ikomoni (late). How I wish you were here in person.

We would, as well, like to dedicate it to Nora Eleanor Brown and Uriah Thomas.

We are also grateful to our eighteen-year-plus assistant, Michell Centeno-Bockarie, who has dedicated her life to the work of God.

We would also like to dedicate this book to prayer warriors and anyone who is struggling with their prayer life. Our prayers are that you discover that praying does not have to be complicated or eloquently spoken. Praying to God can be a casual conversation.

As you read and enjoy this book, remember to share the word that casual prayers are effective. Although prayer can be fun and whimsical, there comes a time when you must pray fervently and prepare yourself for spiritual battle.

Contents

Foreword 1

Casual but Effective Prayers will get you motivated and excited to pray and will give you a deeper understanding of spiritual darkness. You will soon discover that learning how to pray casual but effective prayers will have you on your way of exalting God in all that you do. No matter what your cultural background or your denomination is, we can all agree on the importance of having a healthy prayer life and that praying strengthens our relationship with Jesus Christ.

One of my favorite prayers in this book is the one that speaks about praying as you are closing or opening the blinds. I love opening the blinds in the morning to allow the sun to warm the house and provide nutrients to my plants. I also love closing the blinds at night to protect our privacy as we are preparing supper or getting ready for bed.

As praying can sometimes be intimidating, these prayers are casual, funny, and easy enough for a child to understand how and when to pray. As a parent, you will begin to teach your children how to pray during cleanup time. Picking up toys or pulling them out to play with will become your special time to teach your little one the importance of thanking God for his or her toys.

When we think of praying, we sometimes think that we are supposed to use elaborate words or go on and on. When you sit down to read your first prayer in this book, I guarantee you that you will immediately come up with your own prayers. After reading this book, I now find myself praying as I am applying my lipstick.

I find myself saying, "God, as I apply this lipstick to my lips for beauty, may You apply Your beautiful truth to my lips."

It is an awesome way to get into the habit of praying.

Just as learning how to pray casual but effective prayers is, it is also important to learn about midnight exchange, spiritual demons, and rules of engagement before coming face-to-face with the enemy. This book will teach you how to prepare yourself for battle.

In the army, we call this type of training the "crawl, walk, run" approach. You will start off crawling as you read this book. By the time you get to the "Midnight Exchange" chapter, you will be running or taking off. During this time of learning, you will begin to hunger for more knowledge on the subjects within this book.

When we pray, this is the most personal way. Ephesians 6:18 reminds us that we should always pray specific prayers, on all occasions, stay alert, and pray for everyone.

I would like to congratulate Dr. Alexander and Dr. Angela for thinking outside the box and offering us all a more creative way to pray and to constantly give thanks to our Alpha and Omega, our Great I AM, and the Creator of us all.

—Dr. Olayinka Olubunmi, EdD, MCE,
American Bible University, Inc.

Foreword 2

If you want to judge this book by the cover, then you may miss the essence of this powerful prayer book called *Casual but Effective Prayers*! Please be patient, explore, and peruse it with the passion of a child of God. Dr. Alexander Ikomoni, a prolific writer, has written many books while more are still in the works. However, none comes close to this classic style of using the instrumentality of simplicity to drive home a carefully thought-out approach to prayers through God's revelation. In other words, we can use familiar, mundane, and terrestrial expressions to forge an understanding of celestial and heavenly nuances.

The tools Dr. Ikomoni recommends for effective prayers are very familiar, ubiquitous, recognizable, simple, and very effective. He draws inspiration from the fact that God uses our cultural, ethnic, and traditional idiosyncrasies to elucidate His messages to His people, teach us what to do, and make it fun and less cumbersome when doing it.

Dr. Ikomoni also offers solutions to those who, due to a lack of staying power in prayers, say, "I don't know how to pray." He puts our minds to rest by noting that the efficacy of a prayer is not necessarily determined by its length or duration. He notes that prayer is not legalism. There is no particular way of praying. We should be able to enjoy praying—praying with anything and everything! He talks about "wound prayers," i.e., using physical wounds and bodily injuries as metaphors for dealing a blow to evil manifestations.

Dr. Ikomoni tells us that we can be an embodiment of "a prayer in motion" by us transmuting our daily activities into prayer activism. Examples: opening a door should instigate a prayer of, "As I open this door, so shall new doors swing open in my life in Jesus's name." Also, you, arranging a room, should elicit a prayer of, "As I am arranging this room, please, Lord, arrange and re-arrange my life," etc.

Though this style of praying appears casual, it is, however, very practical and effective. Dr. Ikomoni enjoins that this style does not preclude a child of God from dedicating special times to go into prayer "explosion."

Dr. Ikomoni also draws our attention to the importance of making a vow. But let me quickly note that God does not need anything from us. When we make a vow in the mile of turbulence, we are setting ourselves up for heaven's intervention. When God asks for something from us, He's setting us up for His blessings.

Dr. Ikomoni gives us examples of the daily occurrences, activities, and objects around us that we can use to stop the devil in his tracks: bridge crossing; sunrise; applying body lotion, cologne, and perfume; newborn babies; driving; steps, escalators, and elevators; window blinds; toilet flushing, etc. I have no doubt that, by reason of the spirit of God, the list will generate a life of its own as fervent readers of this book will become innovative in elongating the list.

Finally, Dr. Ikomoni admonishes us to be circumspect in the use of spoken words. This is in tandem with God's biblical injunction: "Death and life are in the power of the tongue" (Proverbs 18:21).

Dr. Ikomoni distinguishes between God's altar and Satan's altar. The devil is pacing to and fro, looking for whom to devour. We must, therefore, continue to pray without ceasing.

This book is unputdownable once you begin to read it! It is my hope that the fervent prayers you, henceforth, render to our Father in heaven, through the inspiration from this book, will avail much. Amen!

—Ambassador Samson Itegboje

Foreword 3

I was privileged to read one of the first drafts of this book, and it was an eye-opener. Drs. Angela and Alexander Ikomoni used the simple, everyday things we know and can relate with to describe precepts and concepts that might have otherwise been difficult to explain.

A friend of mine once told me that everything forms prayer points for her, whether good or bad. This book, *Casual but Effective Prayers*, explains how that can be done, making a habit of prayer on the move, praying for any and everything, big or small, significant or otherwise. This book opens your mind to things that, ordinarily, would have gone unnoticed. It encourages you not to wait for one big-prayer hour but to take advantage of the little seconds, opportunities, and occurrences of everyday events as they pass by.

When we remember that our physical world is shaped and controlled in the spiritual realm, the need to command each day, hour, minute, and second in prayers becomes imperative. This book gives you the blueprint of how to say prayers that are *casual* and yet very *effective*.

—Sharon Osadebamwen

Introduction

God told Jeremiah in Jeremiah 18:2–6,

> "Arise and go down to the potter's house, and there I will cause you to hear My words." Then I went down to the potter's house, and there he was, making something at the wheel. And the vessel that he made of clay was marred in the hands of the potter; so, he made it again into another vessel, as it seemed good to the potter to make. Then the word of the LORD came to me, saying, "O house of Israel, can I not do with you as this potter?" says the LORD. "Look, as the clay is in the potter's hand, so are you in My hand, O house of Israel."

> Son of man, write down the name of the day, this very day the king of Babylon started his siege against Jerusalem this very day. And utter a parable to the rebellious house, and say

to them, thus says the LORD God, "Put on a pot, set it on, and also pour water into it. Gather pieces of meat in it, every good piece, the thigh and the shoulder. Fill it with choice cuts; take the choice of the flock. Also pile fuel bones under it, make it boil well, and let the cuts simmer in it." Therefore, thus says the LORD God, "Woe to the bloody city, to the pot whose scum is in it, and whose scum is not gone from it! Bring it out piece by piece, on which no lot has fallen."

Ezekiel 24:2–6

The word of the LORD came to me, saying, "Son of man, behold, I take away from you the desire of your eyes with one stroke; yet you shall neither mourn nor weep, nor shall your tears run down. Sigh in silence, make no mourning for the dead; bind your turban on your head, and put your sandals on your feet; do not cover your lips, and do not eat man's bread of sorrow." [...] So, I spoke to the people in the morning, and at evening my wife died; and the next morning I did as I was commanded. And the people said to me, "Will you not tell us what these things signify to us, that you behave so?" Then I answered them, "The word of the LORD came to me, saying, 'Speak to the house of Israel, thus says the Lord God, "Behold, I will profane my sanctuary, your arrogant boast, the desire of your eyes, the delight of your soul; and your sons and daughters whom you left behind shall fall by the sword. And you should do as I have done; you shall not cover your lips nor eat man's bread of sorrow. Your turbans shall be on your heads and your sandals on your feet; you shall neither mourn nor weep, but you shall pine away in your iniquities and mourn with one another."'"

Ezekiel 24:15–23

God uses elements, items, objects, situations, experiences, culture, native languages, and backgrounds to speak to us in ways we can understand. God is contextual. He will not speak to you from a Greek culture if you are an African. God understands how the meaning varies from one person to another, from culture to culture, home to home, and family to family. Africans pride themselves on using their natural God-given "cutleries" and often lick their fingers when they are enjoying the food. To the English man, it is an "eek" moment.

God knows these things and understands what is important to you. He knows us more than we know ourselves.

God knows our customs and beliefs. He understands our uniqueness; after all, He created us. God ministers to us from our level of understanding, background, and culture and by using objects and things that we are familiar with.

God knew that Jeremiah understood the purpose of clay and the duties of a potter. God would not have used such allegories to speak to Jeremiah if he were not familiar with them.

Therefore, when we speak to God, we should speak to Him with simple prayers. It is not the eloquence or repetition of words that gets God's attention. We don't have to try to prove that we can pray or that we are anointed to pray. The Bible condemns this behavior in the book of Matthew 6:7, "And when you pray, do not use vain repetitions as the heathen do. For they think that they will be heard for their many words."

Use allegories to make your point clear, but only use objects that you are familiar with. God is an omniscient, omnipotent, and omnipresent—all-knowing, all-powerful, all-seeing—and an "all-wise" God. He knows you. He knows your language, background, culture, and what you are familiar with.

Don't think He does not know your voice or what you know. He knows everything! He knows your mind. Speak (pray) to Him in your understanding—allegorically, illustratively, and continually.

I Don't Know How to Pray

In my thirteen years of ministry, I have come across many who will say to me, "I don't know how to pray. When I go before God, I have no words. I am short of words; I say something for a few seconds and have nothing else to say, and I stop praying." If we can speak to our spouses, friends, and children, argue for so long and be not short of words to tell all those stories, we can speak and pray to God easily.

Many books have been written on how to pray. Sometimes, those books complicate the issue more.

In my early days of Christianity, I remember speaking to my pastor, Bishop Devon Dixon, in New York, about praying over a meal. The best and most effective way to pray, as we discussed, is to quote the Scriptures and pray the Scriptures.

But over the years, I found out that praying is not legalism; praying the Scriptures is good, but it is not compulsory; you can simplify prayers and simplify living. There is grace and mercy; there is no one way to pray. "Die by fire, Holy Ghost fire"—these styles of praying are all good but not the ultimate. It is not the only way. Make praying easy; enjoy praying.

Billy Graham defined *prayer* as a spiritual communication between man and God, a two-way relationship in which man should not only talk to God but also listen

to Him. Prayer to God is like a child's conversation with his father. It is natural for a child to ask his father for the things he needs or just share his day.

Praying is a conversation between you and your Father. Pray in season and out of season, pray continually, pray twenty-four seven. In simple words, talk to your Daddy about anything and everything. Talk to Him always. So, the assignment is to simplify praying and prayers. We can call it "praying made easy." Let us laugh and pray, enjoy praying, and not make praying cumbersome because it is not.

God is always by your side, walking with you, watching you, guiding and directing you, so talk to Him. Show Him things, point things out to Him, tell Him what you think and how you feel, and He will begin to talk back to you.

The Bible admonishes us to pray in season and out of season, but how? I have studied leaders and great men of God like John Wesley, who prayed every time. How do you pray every time? How do you pray in season and out of season? How can you pray continually? These were some of my questions in the seminary. How do you pray when you have to take your shower? How do you "pray always" when you have to eat? How do you "pray always" when you have to go to school? How do you pray continually when you have to go to work and even go dancing and be intimate with your spouse and have an intimate moment with your family? How do you do that? I was thirsty and hungry, and I wanted to find answers.

John Wesley's style gave me the first insight. Praying corporately is a good way to keep your prayer life active. That is why we have a prayer line, which is prayed every three hours round the clock. I realized that I am more motivated to pray around people than to spend time in individual prayers unless there is a burning sensation—meaning something is going on, and I need to spend special time with God.

Praying individually was also practiced by John Wesley. I found it very tasking to stay before God in prayers for more than fifteen minutes. Unless it is a serious situation or by the auctioning of the Holy Spirit, there has to be another way of communicating with my Father. Having and keeping to a devotional time was something that I also adopted. John Wesley read and wrote during his devotions as the Spirit gave him inspiration, and till today, after decades, I enjoy worshiping, praying, reading my Bible, and just writing as the Holy Spirit gives me inspiration. I can do that for hours and don't want to stop. But duties call, and I have to stop to attend to other things.

John Wesley also prayed in the spirit. Praying in the spirit, the way I understood it from John Wesley, is not just speaking in tongues but praying inside. And that I tried to do too but had many distractions.

I also studied the mountain-of-fire prayer style, which, by itself, is work, real sacrifice but very fulfilling. The mountain-of-fire prayer style is a result of heavy demonic oppression, and if you do not fight back with every ammunition available, they will destroy you, your home, and your children. For we do not wrestle against flesh and blood but against principalities, powers, wickedness in high places, rulers of darkness, so they are not playing with us. This style of prayer we call *warfare*; we will treat it better in part B under "Midnight Exchange."

I was still not satisfied with my prayer life. I spent about an hour every day in devotion, praises, prayers, studying and writing. Every three hours, we prayed on the prayer line round the clock, and that was good; it kept me in prayer, and when I could not pray, there was someone else praying for me. It is a fulfilling feeling to know that prayers are being rendered continually on my behalf by my praying team, and I am grateful to them. That was not still enough. I developed the habit of waking up at 3 a.m. for prayers (though not faithfully), which was one of our prayer-line times, and I would stay up till 6 a.m., the next prayer-line time. I tried to praise, worship, study the Word and write as much as I could, and I still felt as if something was missing from the consistency of my prayer life.

I was then reminded of a prophet friend. He always called me his "big brother" and nicknamed me "chairman." "Chairman," as he uses it to address me, is a sign of respect and love. He would always pray with elements, anything and everything. He would say, "Take honey and taste it, and he will say, "Pray, as the honey is sweet, that so shall your life be sweet." He would say, "Pray, as the sun is shining, that so shall your life shine."

Those words kept coming back to me, and I said, "That is it. This way, you can pray in season and out of season"—praying with everything, praying with anything, praying nonstop, praying when eating, praying even when running, like, "As I am running, let my life go faster," praying with driving, like, "This car is going fast, so shall my life go fast and faster without delays."

I began to pray with everything: "As I open this door, so shall new doors swing open in my life in Jesus's name." "As I am arranging this room, please, Lord, arrange and rearrange my life in Jesus's name." These are casual prayers but effective. They gave me fulfillment in my prayer life. So, I have my devotions, individual prayer time, and personal devotion. I have my midnight prayer time and warfare prayer time, and I have my every-three-hour prayer line, which is corporate prayer life, and then praying with everything throughout the day gives me completion and satisfaction of praying in season and out of season, a sense of fulfillment.

I pray that these few lines will help your prayer life get better and stronger, praying casually but effectively.

Part A.

Casual but Effective Prayers

CHAPTER 1

Casual Prayers That Work

Have faith in God. For assuredly I say to you, whoever says to this mountain, "Be removed and be cast into the sea," and does not doubt in his heart but believe that those things he says will be done. He will have whatever he says. Therefore, I say to you, "Whatever things you ask when you pray, believe that you can receive them, and you will have them."

Mark 11:22–24

Can't Use What You Don't Have

Satan and his agents are strong, but the ultimate power belongs to God. Satan comes to steal, kill, and destroy. You cannot bind a strongman unless you are stronger. No matter how much iron you pump, you cannot bind the strongman in the physical sense.

We need a higher power than Satan and his agents if we are going to overcome. Matthew 28:18 records, "And Jesus came and spoke to them, saying, 'All authority has been given to Me in heaven and on earth.'"

Philippians 2:9–11 states,

> Therefore God also has highly exalted Him and given Him the name, which is above every name, that at the name of Jesus, every knee should bow, of those in heaven and of those on earth, and of those under the earth, and that everything should confess that Jesus Christ is Lord to the glory of God the Father.

To destroy these ugly, terrible, and horrific demons ravaging your life, you need to use the power that is higher than they are. All power has been given to Jesus. Therefore, Jesus has stronger and higher powers than any demon. Use the "Jesus" power to bind the strongman and not to let him ravage your life. There is no other name than that of Jesus given to man for salvation. Attach yourself to that power. It is the power of Jesus, and it is free.

To get that free power, we need to follow Romans 10:9–10,

> If you confess with your mouth the Lord Jesus and believe in your heart that God has raised Him from the dead, you will be saved. For with the heart, one believes unto righteousness and with the mouth, confession is made unto salvation.

So, first, put on the helmet of salvation before access can be granted. A sinful life cannot offer acceptable prayers unto God. You must purify yourself of all iniquities of the mind and body.

On our own, we can never be pure. Jesus paid the ultimate sacrifice by dying on the cross for our sins. Jesus, who knew no sin, became sin for us so that we could have access to the Father. Therefore, we are God's righteousness in Christ Jesus. Jesus is the "door," and no one can come to the Father but through Him. Jesus, who knew no sin, became dirty with our sins so we could have access to the Father. So, ask anything in His name, and it shall be given to you.

Power in the Name of Jesus

John 10:7–10 says,

> Then Jesus said to them again, "Most assur-
> edly, I say to you. I am the Door of the Sheep.
> All who ever came before Me are thieves and
> robbers, but the sheep did not hear them.
> I am the door! If anyone enters by Me, He
> will be saved and will go in and out and find
> pasture. The thief does not come except to
> kill, steal, and destroy. I have come that they
> may have life, and that they may have it more
> abundantly.

John 1:4–5a says, "In Him was life, and the life was
the light of men. And the light shines in the darkness
[…]."

Jesus is our advocate and our high priest! To go into
a house, we must go through a door that is, most times,
locked. Jesus is the door; salvation is the key that un-
locks the door to bliss and victory here on the earth
and in eternity. Ask anything in Jesus's name. Without
His name, you are just babbling. Learn how to use the
name! There is power in the name of Jesus.

Prayer is talking to God and God talking back to you.
It is not that hard. It is a two-way conversation. It is

no different from talking with your spouse, neighbors, grocer, doctor, or people on the street. You talk to them, and they talk back to you. Sometimes, they may do all the talking, and you listen, or vice versa. Don't worry about who is talking more; just be in the conversation.

The same thing applies when you are praying. Talk to God, tell Him what you want, tell Him all about your troubles, and tell Him whatever you like or don't like. Pour out your heart, and He will talk back to you. You might be wondering how you will hear Him, but in time, you will learn to recognize His voice. He will not only talk back to you but listen to you, answer your request, and meet your every need.

Casual Conversations

Sometimes, we make easy things difficult, and that prevents many people from trying. The Bible says that God is omniscient. God is ever-present. He is in your car, bedroom, bathroom, and workplace. There is nowhere you can go that He is not present. The psalmist asked the question in Psalm 139:7–11,

> Where can I go from Your Spirit? Or where can I flee from Your presence? If I ascend into heaven, You are there; If I make my bed in hell, behold, You are there. If I take the wings of

the morning and dwell in the uttermost parts of the sea, even there Your hand shall lead me, and Your right hand shall hold me, [...] even the night shall be light about me.

So, you see, He is everywhere, and He hears everything. Talk to Him. Whether casually, formally, or informally—just talk. God watches your every action. When you speak, He listens. When you are gossiping, He hears that too. Whether you are talking with your friends, arguing with your spouse, or showing or talking hatred, He sees and hears it all. He knows your very next move. He knows the thoughts of your heart and can even read your intentions.

So, be careful about your heart condition. What comes out of your mouth is as important as what is in your heart. Jesus said, "Out of the abundance of your heart, the mouth speaks" (Luke 6:45, paraphrased).

When you take time for God, that is great; it is commendable, and Jesus loves it. You may not have a lot of time to dedicate to praying, especially during the days when you are busy at work. Do not wait for that great moment to pray. Take every opportunity to do it because He is listening.

Yes, you can talk to God at any time. You don't have to wait for the church doors to open or for prayer meetings to pray. You can talk to God at any time of the day or night. God is always listening, so ensure that your conversations with others are pure. We should season our tongues with salt and be a light in the darkness. Let your thoughts and deeds be acceptable in the sight of God.

Vows

Always make a vow to God and yourself. In desperate and trying circumstances, make a vow. The Ammonites attacked Israel while Jephthah was a judge of the country. The Bible states that Jephthah pleaded with the king of Ammon to withdraw from the attack, saying, "I have not wronged you. I have not sinned against you. Withdraw the attack" (Judges 11:27, paraphrased).

The Ammonite king did not heed his words, so Jephthah turned to God and made a vow.

> And Jephthah made a vow to the LORD, and said, "If you will give the Ammonites into my hand, then whatever comes out from the doors of my house to meet me when I return in peace from the Ammonites shall surely be the LORD'S, and I will offer it up as a burnt offering."
>
> Judges 11:30–31

The Lord honored the vow and delivered the people of Ammon into Jephthah's hands.

In Judges 11:34–35, we see a return of a warrior fulfilling his vow:

> When Jephthah came to his house at Mizpah, [...] his daughter coming out to meet him with timbrels and dancing: and she was his only child. Besides her, he had neither son nor daughter. And it came to pass when he saw her, he tore his clothes and said, "Alas, my daughter! You have brought me very low. You are among those who trouble me. For I have given my word to the LORD, and I cannot go back on it."

Vows move the hand of God, but you must be very careful when making them. Only make those vows you can keep.

Ecclesiastes 5:4–6 says,

> When you make a vow to God, do not delay it; for He has no pleasure in fools. Pay what you have vowed. It is better not to vow, than to vow and not pay. Do not let your mouth cause your flesh to sin, nor say before the messenger of God, that it was an error.

We used to make vows in the older days, saying, "God, if You give me this girl, I will never chase another again." Or "Lord, if You let me pass this exam, I will serve You forever."

We kept some of the vows but forgot others. Mercy, Lord!

The Word of God says that the Lord has no pleasure in fools. Do not let your mouth lead you into sin. Do not say that your vow was a mistake. Do not provoke God to anger. Much dreaming and many words are truly meaningless. Fear God and keep your vows, and He will always fight for you.

Write Your Prayers and Thoughts Here

CHAPTER 2

Body, Mind, and Spirit Prayers

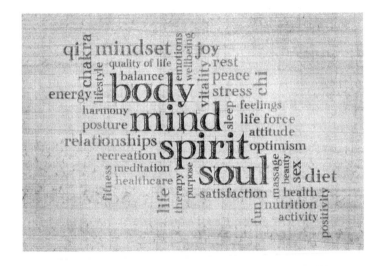

Praying is a way of life, a daily exercise that involves all of your being. Praying can be done as you go about your daily activities.

*B*ath *Prayers*

When you take a bath, you cleanse yourself of accumulated dirt. You use soap to clean every inch of dirt on your body. You use a sponge and a scrub brush to ensure that no dirt remains on your body. You scrub your ears, feet, hair, and the rest of your body to make sure that you are clean and fresh. Some people take a bath twice a day, while others bathe just once per day. I prefer to bathe twice per day.

I am from Nigeria, and we normally bathe in the mornings. Bathing in the mornings became customary for me. I cannot leave the house without taking a good shower.

In America, it is normal to bathe children at night. At first, I could not understand this practice. I soon realized why it made a lot of sense for some children to bathe at night. Many children leave for school very early in the mornings, so it is wiser to bathe at night.

It is cold outside during the fall and winter months. If you take a bath and go outside during the cold seasons, you will likely catch a cold. It is, therefore, better to bathe in the evening when you are home and warm. It does not matter when you bathe, but you should do that at least once per day, preferably twice.

As you bathe, pray that anything that is not of God is washed away. Wash away any sin, anything that makes you smell or feel dirty. Wash away anything that humiliates you. Let negative rumors be washed away in the mighty name of Jesus. Pray to God to make you whole, clean, and better.

Do not take this for granted. Form a good prayer habit. Pray the same prayer when you are bathing your children: "I remove from my child any curse, blemish, and attack that the enemy has put on him [or her]. I wash away any stain or stigma from my child in Jesus's name."

Shower Prayers

Shower times are a good opportunity to make prayer investments in your life. So, never miss the opportunity to worship God. As you are taking a shower, use this time to pray. Pray that every issue in your life, every worry and struggle be washed away in the name of Jesus Christ of Nazareth. Do it as often as you can.

Body-Lotion Prayers

A body lotion is a moisturizer and a protector that keeps skin supple and youthful. It combats dryness that often makes skin look older. Body lotions smooth and soothe the skin. Body lotions delicately scent the skin and prolong summer glow. We lotion ourselves every day. Some people do that once a day, while others do so more often. We apply lotion to our hands when we wash them and when they feel dry or look ashy.

Use this frequent exercise to pray: "As I am applying this lotion to my body, as this lotion is covering my skin, Lord, cover me with Your blood. In fact, I turn this lotion into the blood of Jesus."

Anoint yourself with the lotion: "I cover my finances with the blood of Jesus. I cover my children with the blood of Jesus. I cover my marriage with the blood of Jesus. I cover all that concerns me with the blood of Jesus. My life shall be scented with the blood of Jesus. My life shall have a summer glow. My life will be supple. My life shall be moisturized with the blood of Jesus."

Body-Parts Prayers

Pray this prayer over your body parts: "God, I thank You that my nose is functioning well. I can smell the food that is cooking and the flowers that are blooming. Thank You that I can see. Thank You for the hair that is covering my head, even if it is thinning. I thank You that I can move my hands. I can lift my hands up to You in prayer. I thank You that, as I got up this morning, my legs are still working. God, let every part of my life function to its full capacity in the name of Jesus."

Please ensure that the body part that you are praying over is functioning to its full capacity. Speak to any part of your body that is not functioning well. Pray that the body part will do what it was created to do.

Speak to whatever is not working well in your life. Your body parts were created to serve God and produce enjoyment. Your body must fulfill its purpose in the name of Jesus.

Waking-Up Prayers

Pray that everything that is good in your life rises just as you wake up each day. Let every good thing in your life wake up to its full potential. Let blessings wake up to serve you. Let favor wake up to your destiny. Let grace follow you wherever you go. Let finances wake up to serve you. Let your children wake up to fulfill their destiny. Let goodness and mercy wake up and follow you all the days of your life. Let your heavens open in Jesus's name.

Wound-Treating Prayers

We, occasionally, have cuts on our bodies. We have deep cuts and injuries from accidents or incidents. We bruise ourselves from carelessness, working too hard, rough play, sports, or physical altercations. Such cuts and wounds must be treated. Where I come from, the home therapy for wounds or cuts is to massage the area with hot water to kill the germs.

Afterward, we apply an ointment, such as bacitracin, to the wound. In America, we visit the doctor for wound care and, sometimes, follow-up with antibiotics.

As you are treating such wounds, begin to pray this prayer: "Father, I am claiming to be healed as I am treating this wound. Treat every wound in my life and bring healing expeditiously. Please heal me wherever I have been wounded physically, spiritually, financially, or matrimonially. Wherever I have been wounded by family members, peers, and coworkers, Lord, treat my wounds, heal my wounds, heal my scars—fix it, Lord. Make me better than before. Let my scars show only as a reminder of who You are and how You healed me. Let the pain of the wounds no longer exist."

Some of us have self-inflicted wounds. Our other wounds were made by someone else or life's circumstances. Pray for God to heal you completely.

Many of us have been wounded by family members, loved ones, church members, or church leaders. Use this opportunity to pray for healing in these areas. Pray that the Father's healing hands touch your wounds. Pray that your wounds heal faster, easier, and earlier than expected.

Some wounds are very deep. Pray for God to reach deep down and bring the healing you need. Other wounds may not be as deep, but ask the Lord to bring healing just the same in the name of Jesus.

Pray as often as you treat your wounds. If you use hot water, ice, cold water, ointment, healing oil, or a soothing lotion, let it be a reminder to tell Jesus to apply what is necessary to bring the expected healing. Pray that God soothes the circumstances, for He is the "balm of Gilead." God is the "lily of the valley," the "bright morning star," the dead raiser, and the sea walker. He is a demon slayer, the Great Physician, Jehovah Jireh, and the great healer. There is none like Him, and there will never be anyone like Him. He will apply a special touch, the needed touch, and the right dosage to heal you.

After the prayer, be thankful for healing even if there is no manifestation in the natural yet. Call those things that are not as if they were: "I thank Jesus for healing me. I bless You, Lord, for my healing. I believe it is done in Jesus's name." Celebrate your healing.

*R*unning *Prayers*

Many people are good runners. I am a good sprinter. In fact, everybody can be a good runner. Sprinting depends upon motivation. It does not matter if you have two left legs or are a wheelchair runner. If someone with a machete or an ax is chasing you with the intent of doing bodily harm, you will be the best runner.

There are demons chasing us with the intention to steal, kill, and destroy. We should run for our dear lives.

When we run, we get to our destination faster than if we were walking. We save time by running, overtake, and get ahead.

As you run, pray that your life experiences accelerate promotions in Jesus's name. Pray that you get to your destination quicker and earlier than expected. When you run, use the opportunity to ask God to empower you for greater speed in the spiritual realm.

Ask Him to empower you for you to escape from every enemy pursuing you—in Jesus's name. Pray that the enemy does not catch you or see your taillight. Pray that the enemy does not even know the direction you have taken. Run from sickness, lack, poverty, chaos, abnormalities, the Jezebel spirit, depression, an evil husband or wife, and Satan and his agents, in Jesus's name.

Cologne and Perfume Prayers

I love colognes and perfumes that are not harsh, fake, and mixed with alcohol. I love a calm, sweet, and well-scented fragrance that speaks of love and heaven. I love fragrances like Cool Water, Boss, Ralph Lauren, and Nautica. I am not trying to advertise any product; I just want to share the few that I have had the pleasure of experiencing.

Pray that your life is as sweet-smelling as the fragrance that you are wearing and that wherever you go, people are drawn to your fragrance. Let your life so shine and glorify your Father, who is in heaven.

Best of all, I have found a sweeter scent. The blood of Jesus is a fragrance that will never wear off, even after you bathe. It smells better than any cologne or perfume. Wherever you go, people will enjoy the fragrance as it leaves behind the smell of grace and mercy that none of us deserve. The great thing is that this fragrance is free; Jesus paid for it all.

It is a gift just for you. The only thing you must do is believe in Jesus Christ as your Lord and Savior. As you spray your cologne, pray that your life is always fragrant. Let your life attract goodness, mercy, and grace. Let your life attract blessings and favor in Jesus's name.

*G*iving-Birth *Prayers*

Giving birth to a baby can be both challenging and exciting. Bringing a bundle of joy into this world is an amazing thing. God has allowed you to bring something from nothing.

Use this blessing as a new prayer point: "As this baby is being born, so shall I give birth to great and life-changing ideas. I shall give birth to new businesses, great visions, and creativity." Pray to God to help you push through and bring them to fulfillment in the physical realm in Jesus's name.

Memory-Lane Prayers

Look back over your life and see what has been going on. Go down memory lane and see if God has done anything for you. Count your blessings and name them one by one. If God saw you through those challenges yesterday, He will do the same today. He is faithful.

We have been in situations that we had no idea how to overcome, but somehow, we came out of them. We miraculously came out, shining as gold that had come out of the furnace. Without a shadow of a doubt, God delivered us. God did it for you yesterday, and He can do it for you today. He is the same God yesterday, today, and forever. He does not change or faint. He is the "Alpha and the Omega, the Beginning and the End" (Revelation 1:8).

He is God all by Himself. He doesn't need anyone to help Him be God. He is the all-sufficient God, so never be afraid to present your situations to Him. That situation that looks insurmountable to you is nothing to Him.

Give it to God in prayer. There is nothing too hard for God. He is the mountain mover, miracle worker, sea walker, and dead raiser. So, remind Him that He did it yesterday and that you know He can do it again. He saw you through yesterday and will see you through today. Let Him know that you have confidence in Him.

Colon-Cleanser Prayers

Sometimes we need laxatives to combat constipation. If laxatives do not work, we use a cleanser. Some people will do a three- or seven-day cleanse to clean out their system.

A good cleanser will scrape out waste that is stuck to the walls of the intestines. Spiritually, there are some things in our lives that are hard to overcome. We must scrape and scrub to get them out. Pray that the Holy Spirit permanently removes anything that is in your life and is not of God.

Ask God to use a spiritual cleanser to cleanse you completely of every cankerworm or locust not easily seen. Pray that God washes you with hyssop and makes you whiter than snow: "Scrub everything out of my life that is not of You so I can fulfill my destiny."

Testimony Prayers

I love testimonies because they show God's awesome power working in our lives. God is still on the throne and can deliver each of us. He is no respecter of persons. What He did for Jack, He will do for Jane, Ajasco, and Peninnah.

Remind God that He is faithful and just. God delivered a man nicknamed Ajasco (me) from shame and disgrace. He was homeless, in the gutter, and had no job. His wife left him, but the Lord restored him. God gave Ajasco a simple idea, and now he is a business owner. The Lord enabled Ajasco to buy a mansion and for his family to return home. Ajasco's story ended with praises unto the Lord.

"Father, look at me: I am Yours also. Please favor me as You have favored Ajasco. God, enlarge my territory as You did for Ajasco. Holy Spirit, intercede on my behalf. Father, restore me as You restored Ajasco. You are the same God; You change not. You are still the God of Ajasco, the God of Alexander, the God of Angela, Abraham, Isaac, and Jacob. Favor me as You favored them; in Jesus's name, amen."

*F*ive-Senses Prayers

The five human senses—hearing, seeing, smelling, tasting, and touching—work hand in hand. Pray that, as your five senses work harmoniously in the physical realm, your spiritual senses will be activated. Pray that your spiritual eyes and ears will be opened so that you may hear the inaudible and see the invisible. Pray that you will have spiritual insight, revelations, words of knowledge, and vision. Pray for your spiritual nostrils to be sensitive enough to determine when heavenly angels or demonic spirits are around. In Jesus's name, amen.

*F*all-and-Stagger Prayers

There are times we stagger when walking. It could be caused by your hitting your foot against a stone or a missed step. I have seen ladies lose their balance because of the high heels that they were wearing. Sometimes, the pointed heel of the shoe will break off and send someone flying across the room. As we get older, many of us become more unstable on our feet. It is easy for us to miss a step, trip over something, and lose our balance.

Anytime you experience such abnormalities, use this opportunity to pray against falling: "Satan, you have lost again. I am stable; I am strong. I will not stumble; I will not fall in my life. I will not fall financially, nor will I fall in my marriage. My ministry will soar, and there will be no going down for me—in the mighty name of Jesus!"

Pray that your home and business will be solid.

Don't take anything for granted. Send anything that is not of God back to the sender to scatter the plans of the enemy. Pray against anything that can make you stagger in life. If you do not pray, you will fall. If you fall, the Bible says that though a righteous may fall, he will surely rise up (Proverbs 24:16).

If you fall, get back up. Pray to God for Him to help you rise higher than before. Pray that God will help you stand up, stronger and better than before.

Dream Prayers

When you dream or have night visions, you should pray for or against them immediately. If the dream is repeated more than twice, it means that it is very serious. You should begin a fast immediately.

I am calling you to prayers and not dream interpretations. If it is a good, sweet, and victorious dream filled with progress, pray that it comes to pass as it has been revealed. If it is a negative dream, cancel it immediately. The enemy is setting you up for disaster. Rebuke him at once.

Speaking-and-Listening Prayers

I like to listen more and speak less. However, I am not always successful at doing this. When you speak less, you appear to be full of wisdom. The Word of God says we are to be quick to listen, slow to anger, and slow to speak (James 1:19).

Some people are good listeners and can hear and understand very clearly. Pray that you will hear the Holy Spirit when He speaks to you. Pray that you will hear God as clearly as you hear the people around you. Pray to be a good listener and doer of the Word of God. Pray that the Holy Spirit will teach you when to talk and when to put a guard on your mouth. Pray that God will control your tongue because the tongue can be unruly and restless, evil, and full of poison. Pray for your tongue to bless and not to curse. Pray that your words will be fitly spoken, like apples of gold in silver settings (Proverbs 25:11).

Even a fool will be deemed wise if he closes his mouth (Proverbs 17:28).

Walking Prayers

The process of walking is putting one leg in front of the other to get you from one point to the other. Today, we are advised to walk daily to keep us healthy.

Turn your walking time into a time of prayer. Pray that there will be no stagnation in your life as you are putting one leg in front of the other. Pray that you will move only forward.

Walking is not as fast as running or driving but is still mobility. Pray for your children, business, ministry, and finances to keep moving forward. Pray daily to experience God's hand upon your life.

Praise Prayers

We were created to worship. In fact, we serve a God who inhabits the praises of His people.

We should form a habit of always praising God. Let everything and anything elicit praise. Give thanks to God whether you receive a gift, your paycheck, or have food on your table. Praise God if you can smell, eat, have the ability of your limbs, or use the bathroom. Worship God for the beauty of His holiness. Just praise Him!

As you praise, turn it into prayer: "Father, I call You blessed! As I am calling You blessed, let my family call me blessed. As I magnify Your name, let my community magnify my name. As I lift You up, Father, let my region and territory lift me up. As I push to do Your will and Your work, let everyone I meet push to do work for me. As I glorify Your name, Father, glorify me, and all the glory shall come back to You in Jesus's name."

Write Your Prayers and Thoughts Here

CHAPTER 3

Transportation Prayers

Moving is a life necessity with its ups and downs, disappointments, delays, and failures. In spite of it all, we possess the ability to overcome any obstacle that comes our way.

*B*ridge-Crossing Prayers

You should use the opportunity to pray any time you are crossing a bridge. Without the bridge, you will be stuck and will face more hardships and delays. You may not be able to get to your destination in a timely manner without a bridge. Bridges are crucial in our journey. Pray that as you are crossing this bridge, there be bridges available in the spiritual realm to cross over to your destiny. As you are crossing this natural bridge, you must also cross over in the spiritual realm. Financially, let there be bridges to get you to your destination. Let this bridge move you from the lower class to the upper class. Let it move you from your singleness (if you want it) to being married. Let it move you from a place of lack to a place of having more than enough. Pray and ask the Father to erect bridges in your life where they are needed. In Jesus's name, amen.

*D*riving Prayers

Driving a vehicle is fun, especially a new sports vehicle. The good thing about driving a vehicle is not just the fun but also the comfort it provides. Riding in a vehicle can sometimes be dangerous because of the person who is driving and other drivers on the road. Driving a vehicle gets you to your destination faster than walking.

31

Pray that as you are driving your vehicle, it gets you to your destination safely. As your vehicle moves forward smoothly, so shall your life move forward smoothly in Jesus's name.

Remember that the spiritual realm controls the natural. If you get hold of the spiritual realm, you will get hold of the natural. The steps of the righteous are ordered by God. Let God Himself direct your life. Let God be in the driver's seat. When God drives your life, nothing can go wrong.

*T**raffic-Jam Prayers*

I do not like traffic jams. Traffic jams hold you up and are chaotic and confusing. When you are in a traffic jam, you are at a standstill or barely moving. Traffic jams lead to delays and possibly missed appointments. Pray against any delays in your life, businesses, or churches. Pray against anything that will bring delay, stoppage, or lateness. We rebuke it in Jesus's name. Rebuke every delay and stoppage in your life. Pray that lack does not stop you, delay you, or humiliate you. Pray that poverty does not stop you and sickness does not halt you. Pray against infirmities. Whenever you are in a traffic jam, use the opportunity to pray for God to clear your way in the natural and in the spiritual. There were times we have prayed this prayer, and God cleared the traffic immediately in the natural as well as in the spiritual.

Red-Light and Stop-Sign Prayers

Red lights mean, "Do not go." When you are in a hurry, red lights can be annoying. Use the opportunity to pray when red lights slow you down. Pray for all the lights to be green so that you can sail through. Pray that whatever is stopping or slowing you down will be removed from your path in the name of Jesus. Pray that the path shall always be open for you. Pray that financial stoppage may be eradicated from your life. Pray that whatever is keeping your marriage from prospering be removed. Rebuke all red lights, stop signs, delays, lack, poverty, and sickness from your life in Jesus's name.

People have been stagnant in their lives and jobs for years. Remember: the enemy is holding you back. The enemy comes to block you and set you back.

Green-Light Prayers

Green lights, yellow lights, and red lights are traffic-control measures. Red light means "do not go"; yellow light means "slow down," and green light means "go." The green light gives you permission and authority to proceed.

Monopoly is a game that my siblings and I played with our mother. My first daughter, Ufuoma, would always win. You are rewarded each time you pass a "go" in Monopoly. The "go" in *Monopoly* is a green light that gives you the authority to continue going forward. You are neither going backward nor going to jail; you can move forward. Pray that as the light turns green, so it will be in the spiritual realm. No stoplights, only green lights in your life, giving you power, authority, and permission to proceed to your destination, in Jesus's name. Pray that there will be no setbacks or delays, only green lights.

Steps, Escalators, and Elevator Prayers

Steps are created to get you to higher levels. Escalators and elevators were created as an alternative to climbing stairs. Whether you climb stairs, take an escalator or elevator, pray that as you are climbing, you will only experience upward mobility in your life. Rebuke any downward movements in your life in Jesus's name.

Airplane Prayers

Airplanes have momentum. It takes me about sixteen to seventeen hours to drive from New York to Atlanta, Georgia. When I'm traveling by plane, it takes just about two hours and fifteen minutes. It would be preposterous to think of walking that distance. Pray that your life will not go into the walking mode when your life should be gaining momentum. Pray that your life will accelerate with the speed of an airplane in your finances, reputation, marriage, and health because you were born as an heir to the King.

The devil is a liar!

It is an error to progress in arithmetic form of $(1 + 1 = 2 + 1 = 3 + 1 = 4 + 1 = 5)$; you shall progress in a geometric form of $(1 + 1 = 2; 2 + 2 = 4; 4 + 4 = 8; 8 + 8 = 16)$.

Pray for a smooth takeoff in your life. In the same way a plane takes off and flies higher, you will also fly higher in Jesus's name.

*B*eautiful-Cars Prayers

There are so many beautiful cars with different designs, capabilities, and manufacturers. I love new cars that are reliable. I detest the struggle and headaches that can come with old cars. Some cars may not be brand-new, but nonetheless, they still look good and run well.

Pray, "As this car is beautiful, let my life, business, and marriage also be beautiful. I do not want my life to be as beat-up as an old car. I do not want my life to have issues like that of an old car with a bad engine. Father, I want my life to run smoothly with no glitches, blemishes, complaints, and nothing missing or broken—in Jesus's name."

Moving Prayers

Moving can be stressful. Moving to a new home, a better house, or a more upscale neighborhood is a blessing and an exciting adventure. Pray, as you are moving to this new house and more upscale neighborhood, that your life, marriage, and job will also move to the next level. Pray that God will move your children or your family members to higher heights, higher than they can ever imagine. Pray for advancement on the job, in your business, financial and spiritual, in the name of Jesus.

Towing-Trucks Prayers

Tow trucks are meant to tow disabled vehicles that are obstructing the way of other vehicles. There are different types of tow trucks. Some have a hook and chain, flatbed, or wheel lift.

Pray that you will not be broken down to a point where someone else will have to drag you along or carry you on their back: "Father, I will not have issues or problems that will require someone else to carry me financially, matrimonially, or otherwise. My life will not have any accidents that will require someone to fix or come to a halt. I will not break down with sickness or disease. My family or my business will not break down spiritually and require towing, in Jesus's name."

Anytime you see a tow truck, pray that the engine and wheels of your life will always be lubricated and ready for life's journey, in Jesus's name.

Write Your Prayers and Thoughts Here

CHAPTER 4

Blockages and Plumbing Prayers

Hindrances, obstacles, barricades, and blockages are life occurrences that must be moved from our path for us to experience a peaceful and prosperous life.

*B*lockage and Plunger Prayers

Sometimes our sinks and toilets get clogged and flood the room, creating a mess. Clogged sinks and toilets are not useable.

We were on vacation at a resort in Orlando, and the entire room stank from a toilet blockage. The blockage flooded the bathroom, so we had to call the maintenance department. Maintenance did not come until 2 a.m. to fix the problem. Afterward, the cleaning crew came to tidy things up.

It is crucial to unblock and unclog for sanitary and health reasons. As you are trying to unclog your toilet, pray that every blockage in your life will be removed. As you clear the system, channel, or tunnel, so shall every system and channel in your life be unblocked. Whatever is blocking your life, pray that it will give way in Jesus's name.

*S*nake-as-a-Plumbing-Tool Prayers

When a liquid plumber or plunger can no longer do the job, it is time to bring in a "snake." A snake is a plumbing tool that is more sophisticated than a plunger or liquid plumber.

Likewise, in our life, certain things have developed strong roots because of the length of time the problem has been left unattended.

Matthew 17:21 reads, "However, this kind does not go out except by prayer and fasting." You must fast and pray to unclog some things in your life. Pray that the Holy Spirit will burn to ashes the root of your problems. Send everything back to the sender. Reverse what the enemy is trying to do in your life. Serve the enemy an eviction notice and marshal him out of your life in Jesus's name.

The Plunger Prayers

The plunger is used to unclog light plumbing problems. It creates an air vacuum that pushes down the substance that is clogging the toilet. Pray that anytime you use the plunger, the Holy Spirit will remove anything that is clogging your destiny.

It is time to call the plumber when neither the plunger, liquid plumber, nor the snake can do the job. It is time to stop trying to fix it yourself. It is time to surrender! Let God know that you need Him and that you cannot fix it on your own. You lack the wisdom, ability, and experience to solve the problem. Tell God that you know that there is nothing too hard for Him to fix. Ask God to fix any area of your life that needs fixing, "Lord, release Your power in my life."

Write Your Prayers and Thoughts Here

CHAPTER 5

Bathroom Prayers

Cleansing and removal of waste are necessary for living, so they are in the spiritual realm.

Restroom-Usage Prayers

Using the restroom is a necessity for us all. It is recommended that we use the bathroom at least once per day, if not three times per day. When you do number one or number two, you are eliminating waste from the body. Waste is toxic, dangerous, and harmful to the body and should not be stored in our body.

Learn to pray with everything. Waste is part of our lives that must be disposed from our bodies. You feel relieved when nature calls and you go to the bathroom to release waste from your body. There is always a sense of release and freedom, a feeling of comfort. Sometimes the pressure is so much that when we release it, we say, "Thank You, Lord." As you advance in age, restroom usage becomes a blessing.

Pray, "Father, as I am using this restroom and all this waste is coming out of me, let every bad thing in my life come out, in the name of Jesus. Every waste, every ugliness, everything that clogs me, everything that is interfering with my comfort—let it come out."

There are some things in our life that will not come out that easily, except by an extra push. Sometimes we take laxatives (fasting) to push them out. Pray, "As I eliminate this waste, if there is any harmful substance in my life, my marriage, my family, or my finances, remove it in Jesus's name." Pray against any clogs in your business or your decision-making process. Ask God to eliminate, remove, excavate, and marshal out any clogs in Jesus's name.

Extraordinary Restroom Prayers

There are times when you take a laxative to push out everything. Sometimes you are so clogged that you need to do a colon cleanse to push everything out. When you go to the bathroom, the smell makes you wish that you were not in the same bathroom with the contents. The smell can also have you wondering if this is coming from you. Pray, "As every ugliness is coming out, Father, let every ugliness in my life come out in the name of Jesus."

Flushing-Toilet Prayers

After using the bathroom, or "dumping," as my son calls it, you need to flush the toilet. Now that the waste is out, it stinks, and the sight of it is not good. Flushing is the process of washing away the waste to an unknown land. A place where it will be buried somewhere, never to return. Pray that as you flush the toilet, you are also flushing the spiritual toilet. Anything in your life that is not of God must be flushed away. Anything in your life that stinks will be flushed away in Jesus's name.

Laxative Prayers

Eating the wrong kinds of food and not drinking enough water can lead to constipation. For those of us who can use the bathroom with ease—thank God. Some people are in serious pain because of irregular bowel movements.

I was rushed to the hospital in pain one night. When the doctor came in, I thought he would say that this was the end for me. Instead, he said I needed to drink more water. Whenever I feel bloated, I take a Smooth Move laxative or drink herbal tea.

My wife loves the herbal stuff. Herbs are healthy for us and prescribed by God. As we eat healthily, use herbal supplements or plants, drink water or coconut water, and eat more vegetables, our days of constipation will be far behind us. Adding more fiber to your diet and having a healthy system will give you the relief that you need. Pray that, as you find relief by eating healthily, your life will become healthier by your eating the Word of God. Your marriage and your finances will become healthier as you follow God's prescription.

Laxatives are important when someone is constipated. Unclogging the pipe is extremely important to our well-being. If it does not happen naturally, you should get extra help to unclog the pipe. Use the workability of a laxative to engage in warfare.

Pray that the Lord will eradicate anything clogging your life. If sin is hiding somewhere, pray for it to come out. If you are struggling with any kind of addiction that is keeping you bloated, pray that it will come out in Jesus's name. Ask God to let you be free of any attachments sent from the enemy. Flush those things out in the name of Jesus.

Write Your Prayers and Thoughts Here

CHAPTER 6

Garbage-Removal Prayers

When garbage is removed, it is removed. It does not make its way back into your house. It is removed permanently. So shall your problems be and never return.

Picking-up-Trash Prayers

It is unsightly to have trash everywhere. In fact, as the adage goes, cleanliness is next to godliness. Make it a habit to always keep your surroundings clean and litter-free.

Whenever you are out walking and see trash, pick it up. In fact, make a habit of carrying a garbage bag with you. This is how you become the solution to a problem. Pray as you are cleaning and picking up this garbage that God will clean all of the garbage that resides in you. Ask God to open your eyes to see the trash that might be hiding in your life and that needs to be picked up and destroyed.

Garbage-Bin and Garbage-Truck-Removal Prayers

I must take out my trash every week for the garbage truck to pick it up. As soon as it is picked up for disposal, it is gone forever. Once the garbage is gone, it will never be redelivered to you. Pray as you are disposing of the garbage that God will also dispose of all your garbage in the name of Jesus, "Lord, as the garbage truck rolls down the road, let the garbage in my life, marriage, finances, business, and my children's lives be rolled away forever. In Jesus's name, amen."

*G*arbage-Disposal Prayers

Garbage is nothing but leftovers or waste that needs to be thrown away. Garbage leaves behind a smell that attracts flies. It is important for us to rid our homes, communities, and surrounding areas of garbage for health reasons. Pray that every spiritual garbage in your life is removed. Everything that is making your life stink—may it be removed permanently, in Jesus's name. Refuse to accept any more waste in your life once you have disposed of that garbage.

Write Your Prayers and Thoughts Here

CHAPTER 7

Turning-on-the-Light Prayers

The true light that gives light to all shines in the darkness.

Turning-Lights-On-And-Off-in-Your-House Prayers

We turn lights on when we enter buildings and turn them off when we leave. Light switches are located near the door for ease of use. When you enter a room, you want to turn the light on quickly so that you won't stumble or fall.

It was so hard to get my son to follow suit. He would leave light switches running all day until I had to threaten to make him pay the bill.

As you are switching the lights on or off, pray and ask God to turn on the light in your life, "Father, as I turn on the lights, I ask that You turn the lights on in the lives of my family, spouse, and business. I am turning on goodness, favor, victory, peace, progress, prosperity, and health in my life in the name of Jesus."

When you turn off the lights, pray, "Father, as I am turning off this light, I am turning off lack, sickness, depression, and poverty in my life. I switch off whatever has not been working for me, in the name of Jesus."

Light-in-the-House Prayers

Upon entering your home, the first thing that you do is to turn on the lights. When you turn on the light, darkness disappears. As darkness disappears when you turn on the light, so shall every darkness in your life. Use this opportunity to ask God to shine a bright light on your life. If your light becomes dim, pray and ask God to brighten it again. Pray, "God, as Your light shines bright, let the brightness shine on my family, children, business, marriage, health, and finances, in the name of Jesus."

Write Your Prayers and Thoughts Here

CHAPTER 8

Commitment and Committed Prayers

Commitment and faithfulness are a life discipline that is cherished by all, including our Maker.

Ring Prayers

I love my wedding ring and was quite frustrated when an uncared-for teenager broke into my house and stole it. This act was a violation of sacredness. My wife had to arrange to purchase a new wedding band for me.

Wedding rings are circular in shape to symbolize a circle that is never-ending. As the circle continues, so shall your marriage and your love for one another. If your wedding ceremony included a ring, use your ring to pray that just as the shape of the ring is unending, so shall your finances be unending. Use the understanding of the circular shape of the ring as a point of prayer.

Teaching Prayers

I am a good teacher who is anointed to teach. Teachers look for ways to impart knowledge with the expectation that the students are receiving the instructions. The hope is that the taught materials are beneficial not only to the students but also to society.

Everyone engages in one form of teaching or the other. Each of us unconsciously engages in teaching every day. You may be anointed to teach, called to teach, or see yourself as a teacher. Nonetheless, you are a teacher. We teach our children and others by our words and actions.

As you are teaching, pray that you are also being taught by the Holy Spirit. Pray that the Holy Spirit will impart knowledge and wisdom to you. Ask the Holy Spirit to illuminate your understanding of what you are teaching. Pray that the Holy Spirit will allow you to become more creative and innovative in your teaching so you can reach corporate America and beyond. Pray that the Holy Spirit will allow you to be the best husband, wife, leader, businessman, and businesswoman.

Doing-Good Prayers

Although goodness will not qualify you as a candidate for heaven, it is good to do good. It is good to bless people, feed the hungry, clothe the naked, and provide shelter for the homeless. Pray that as you are doing good to others, God will cause people to do good to you also, in Jesus's name. Pray that even heaven will favor you, in Jesus's name.

Council-and-Meetings Prayers

A council is a group of persons who come together to brainstorm and make decisions. People meet and discuss plans on how to do business and move forward in life. Just as we come together, so does the enemy. The enemy meets and discusses ways to make your life miserable, destroy your home, and take your children from you. The enemy will discuss how to make you lose your job or business, bankrupt you, and make you a beggar and a loner. His goal is to make you die alone and ultimately get you to miss heaven and suffer in hell.

Pray that any meeting that is not of God, any ungodly council and counsel, utterances, incantations, divinations, pronouncements, and discussions about you may be destroyed. Their plans against you should come to naught, in Jesus's name.

People meet in boardrooms, living rooms, restaurants, and parks. The enemy meets in covens, on treetops, under the earth, and in the sea. Pray that wherever they are meeting, the Holy Ghost will release fire to burn and destroy their gatherings and meetings, in Jesus's name. So, when you see meetings taking place in restaurants, parks, boardrooms, and churches, let this be a reminder to pray this prayer and release the Holy Ghost's fire to burn the enemy to ashes.

Church-Cleaning Prayers

At the beginning of my ministry, I would clean the house of the Lord alone. I was the janitor, organizer, Sunday school teacher, Wednesday Bible studies teacher, custodian, door opener, usher, preacher, treasurer, secretary, and praise and worship leader. All these experiences have caused me to love taking care of the house of the Lord. It feels good to clean the house of the Lord. In fact, cleaning, in general, is a good thing. Cleaning brings joy and happiness and leads to good health. For those involved in the sanctification of the house of God: I applaud and encourage you to do so with a joyful heart. God will be your rewarder! Pray as you clean the house of God that God will clean your house. Pray that God will clean and rid the filth out of your life and the lives of your family. Ask Him to cleanse the filth of your body, soul, and spirit. Ask the Lord to fix them for you.

*T*ime-of-Arrival Prayers

We need to be time conscious in our lives. Western culture is very conscious of time and respects the time of others. However, other cultures are not as concerned or bothered about time.

Make it a point of duty not to arrive at arranged meetings late. As you arrive early, use this time to pray, "Father, as I am early to this appointment, let me also achieve early success, wealth, promotion, and a timely blessing. Let me be the first in my industry to succeed, be blessed, and be promoted. Let me arrive at my destination early, in the name of Jesus."

If you are late, rebuke and vow never to be late in having children, marrying, or becoming a millionaire. Pray that your hands are blessed and that you are blessed in your comings and your goings. Most importantly, pray that you will know God earlier than appointed and that you will do the will of the Father earlier than appointed.

Write Your Prayers and Thoughts Here

CHAPTER 9

In-Season and Out-of-Season Prayers

For everything, there is a season.

*P*raying *Against a Hard Life*

Sometimes life can be hard. Although you try and try, nothing seems to be working, but you must keep trying. You cannot give up. You are already defeated if you do not try. If you fail, do it again. If you fall, get up. You keep trying and keep going until you succeed. Pray against hard life every chance you get. Whenever you step on hard concrete, pray that your life will never experience hardships, in Jesus's name. When you step on succulent objects like a well-padded carpet or foam, pray that your life will be softer, better, and easier than anyone can imagine.

*E*nd-*of-Month/Year Prayers*

God's covenant with day and night is that the night must give way to the day. The night has been commanded to come to an end. It cannot be changed. The day must shift, giving way to the night.

So, it is with the last day of the month and the last month of the year. The prayer point is the day, month, and year are to end without question. Every difficult problem, storm, dark hour, sickness, and lack must come to an end. Pray against poverty, oppression, disappointment, and depression. Pray against sleeplessness, tears, mourning, ashes, pain, and sorrow. All these things must come to an end in your life, in the name of Jesus.

Pray this prayer: "Father, as this month is coming to an end, let there be an end to all my pain and struggles. As this day is coming to an end, anything that went wrong must also come to an end. As this year is ending, it is also the end of all my failures and disappointments. Let every disappointment, failure, mistake, shame, and temptation come to an end in my life in the name of Jesus. Whatever is wrong must come to an end. I put a stop to all wars, chaos, and confusion in my life.

"As a new chapter is opening, a new day, month, and year, there will be newness in my life, in the mighty name of Jesus the Christ. Whatever is not working will begin to work for me. There shall be open doors of possibilities, new doors of appointments, and new doors in every area of my life, in Jesus's name. Turn every struggle into progress, every darkness into light, every mourning into joy, every disappointment into appointments, every sickness into good health, and every failure into success, in Jesus's name."

Nine-Eleven Prayers

Pray against any emergencies or any unforeseen contingencies. When the date is 9/11, rebuke and bind any emergencies for the day. When the time is 9:11, rebuke and bind this time for one minute. Refuse and reject all emergencies and any attacks from the enemy. Send back all attacks to the enemy in the name of Jesus.

Upside-Down Rebuking Prayers

There are times in our lives or in our daily activities when we are so busy that we are not cognizant of our actions. We put things on wrongly, or we put them in the wrong places. Sometimes we put things upside down or backward. When you notice such wrong actions, immediately rebuke them. Do not take it for granted. Pray that your life will not be upside down. Pray that your life will always be right in the name of Jesus.

Sometimes we put our clothes on backward. This normally happens because we are in a hurry or not paying attention. If you put your clothes on inside out or backward, pray immediately that your life will not be upside down. Pray that your finances will not be upside down. Pray that your life will continue to move forward and not backward, in Jesus's name. Your life will have no reverse gear; it is forward and upward only, with no backwardness, in Jesus's name. Your prayer life will not be upside down or backward. Your prayer life will grow stronger. Pray in season and out of season.

*P*ray-without-Ceasing *Prayers*

The Bible admonishes us to pray without ceasing, and that means to pray continually. Praying without ceasing can be a struggle for those who do not understand. A sustained prayer life is required for victory. The enemy is like a roaring lion seeking whom he will devour (1 Peter 5:8). He takes advantage of every loophole in your life. Since he comes like a thief to strike, you must be on your guard and ready for battle.

The weapons of our warfare are not carnal but mighty through God for pulling down strongholds. Use prayer as your weapon.

> For we do not wrestle against flesh and blood, but against principalities, against powers, against the rulers of the darkness of this age, against spiritual hosts of wickedness in the heavenly places.
>
> Ephesians 6:12

You must constantly be on your guard. You cannot put your hands down for one minute. If you put your hands down, the spiritual Muhammad Ali will rearrange your face and destroy you. Prayer is a very powerful and important weapon.

We encourage you to pray without ceasing. You can be as busy as a bee, but you still need to take time out to pray. It is the will of the Father for us to pray without ceasing; according to 1 Thessalonians 5:16–18, "Rejoice always, pray without ceasing. In everything give thanks. For this is the will of God in Christ Jesus for you."

Casual but Effective Prayers was born so that you do not stop praying.

Court-Cases Prayers

I do not like the legal system. I was poised to be an attorney until God shifted my focus. I am a fighter physically and spiritually. I hate oppression and injustice of any kind. I will fight with every inch and molecule in me to stand against oppression and injustice. After years of being in and out of the courts, I dislike our very unfair legal system. If you do not have enough money, you will not get fair representation in court. Even with enough money, sometimes, cases are won not on merits but on technicalities in America. An offender can easily go free. Banks go scot-free after committing atrocities because they have the best lawyers. My wife always says that poverty is a crime.

The rich get away with so much, and "godfather" criminals or connections get cases won.

As we have natural courts on the earth, there are courts in heaven where cases are heard. It is important to take your case to the courts of heaven. Heaven's courts are fair and just with a good attorney who has already paid the price for you. He has a direct connection with the judge, so you cannot lose your case. You cannot be found guilty if you are covered by the precious blood of Jesus. As the judge rules in the natural, so the Master Judge rules in the heavens. He will always rule in your favor in Jesus's name. Believers receive an automatic grace.

The Bible says in John 3:18, "He who believes in Him is not condemned; but he who does not believe, is condemned already, because he has not believed in the name of the only begotten Son of God." The enemy cannot do anything to you unless they find you guilty in the spiritual realm. Present your case in the heavenly courts first so that Jesus can fight for you.

Please note that you have already won the case. Jesus has already handed the victory to you. He is the winner. Even before you were accused, the judge had no other choice than to acquit you.

Goodness and mercy shall follow you all the days of your life (Psalm 23:6). To reiterate: the idea is to pray with everything and anything. It is a reminder to pray always.

I was in court recently and saw people with different cases. The enormous power placed on the judge is unbelievable. People's lives and futures are in the hands of the judge. I pray that your lives and futures will be not in the hands of any earthly judges but those of Jesus, covered by His precious blood. Pray that no man will have the power over your life. Pray that only Jesus will be seated on the judgment seat in your life. He and only He will render the verdict. If you believe and live right, the verdict will always be in your favor. As the earthly judge is giving the verdict to acquit you, pray that every verdict in your life in the spiritual realm shall be the same. You are free to go; you are not guilty, in Jesus's name. He has paid it all for you already.

*B*reakables or Life-Shattering Prayers

Sometimes in life, we break objects. We break drinking glasses, bottles, or glassware by mistake or by design. Some things are so broken that they cannot be glued back together.

Humpty Dumpty had a great fall, and all the king's men, including Satan, could not put Humpty Dumpty back together again. If you break or shatter anything, pray that as this glass or ceramic plate fell and broke into pieces, so shall every problem, obstacle, or hindrance in your life be broken and shattered, in Jesus's name. Pray that it cannot be put back together.

Sometimes you must purposely break some things from your life in Jesus's name. Just take the glass and shatter it. As you are doing this, pray that every ugliness, disappointment, divorce, lack, poverty, generational curse, addiction, and sickness in your life will be broken. Break every chain, every stronghold, and anything that is holding or bounding you. Break it in Jesus's name. Whatever is hard, whatever is not going too well, must be broken in Jesus's name.

Shattering-of-Ware Prayers

I hate it when glassware falls out of my hand and breaks. I was trying to clean a teacup recently, and it accidentally fell from my hands and broke. I was muttering about it, and the Holy Spirit reminded me to turn it into prayer. I prayed that every problem and evil attack in my life would be destroyed completely.

Use such circumstances as an opportunity to pray so that every ugliness in your life will be broken. In fact, take breakable ware and shatter it into pieces that cannot be put back together. Pray, "As this breakable ware is shattered, every problem in my life will also be shattered in the mighty name of Jesus."

Tree Prayers

I currently live in Georgia, and there are trees everywhere. Some of the trees are well rooted and are hard to remove, while others are easy to uproot. My pool was not attended to for a while, and some little pine trees began to grow. The contractor who we hired to restore the pool literally plucked the trees out of the pool. The little pine trees were easy to uproot, but the border trees are well rooted because they have been there for years.

Our prayer lives should be as rooted and firm as the border trees: "Father, as this tree has roots deep down in the ground and is unshakable, let my life grow so strong with roots that also cannot be moved. Let me be unshakable irrespective of the storms. Let me be as strong as the iroko and oak trees, in Jesus's name."

*F*lies-and-Fleas-Swatting Prayers

Flies and fleas are annoying as they buzz around, sometimes unseen. They carry diseases and germs, and if the wound is left untreated, flies and fleas can cause an infestation. I hate to see them, especially when I am eating. During summer barbecues, they can become burdensome. You dare not open your doors without a screen during the hot summer months. Once the doors are open, they immediately come into your home.

Flies and fleas were very common at my old house. They were everywhere even though it was a nice middle-class neighborhood. It is not unheard of to swat and kill around ten to twenty flies on a bad day. My house is always clean and sparkling. This was one of the reasons why I was attracted to my wife. She keeps everything clean and in order. The flies still come, although the house is always clean.

I used to live close to a lot of woods, but no swamps were close to the house. We were constantly buying flyswatters.

Some flies stay in their own territory to avoid being swatted, but others venture out and pay the price. Pray that God would give you a Holy Ghost swatter to swat every demon that is flying, buzzing, and disturbing you. Pray that you will see them coming and destroy them in Jesus's name. Pray to be sensitive to your surroundings and ready to swat them before they come to kill, steal, and destroy you. Destroy them before they destroy you. Pursue them before they pursue you. Torment them before they torment you, and swat them before they swat you.

Wipes-and-Sanitizing Prayers

Wipes are used to clean babies, the sticky hands of children, and office spills. Sanitized wipes were a necessity during the Coronavirus pandemic, but they were scarce and expensive. There are various brands of wipes, and some are more effective than others, but there are no wipes that are better than the Holy Ghost wipes. Pray that the Holy Spirit will wipe away every mess in your life in the name of Jesus. Let the Holy Spirit be your wipes. Always engage Him to wipe every mess out of your life and the lives of your loved ones in Jesus's name.

*T*ree-Roots Prayers

The root of a tree provides needed nourishment and support for that tree. By the same token, every persistent, consistent, and long-lasting problem has roots. The problems will remain until you cut off the roots.

Sometimes we treat the headache, which is a symptom of a more serious problem. The root of the problems must be dealt with to overcome the challenge. Pray that the Holy Ghost will burn to ashes any root of your problem. Ask the Holy Spirit to dry up any sources of nourishment for your problems. Whatever is feeding the problems must dry up in Jesus's name.

*I*roning-Clothes Prayers

An iron is a heated element that is used to remove wrinkles from clothing. When we iron our clothes, it gives a good impression. There is a new fashion trend today where anything goes. In my opinion, wrinkled clothes are equal to laziness.

Ironing was one of my chores when I was growing up. I am thankful today for the training to properly iron clothes. I guess this is one reason why I iron my jeans. My son laughs and asks, "Who irons their jeans?" I just look at him and say, "I do."

As you are ironing your clothes, ask God to iron out any wrinkles in your life. If there are any wrinkles in your character, reputation, marriage, children, business, or finances, pray that God will get rid of them in the name of Jesus.

Write Your Prayers and Thoughts Here

CHAPTER 10

Food Prayers

Use food to form a prayer habit.

*A*bundance *Prayers*

There are times in our lives when God blesses us with so much. The shoe closet is full; the clothes closet has no space for new ones, and the refrigerator is full. It is an abundance, a period of overflow, blessings untold. Many of us do not even realize that it is a period of more than enough. In my house, we have a gigantic fridge on the first floor, a freezer in the garage, and another good-size fridge in the basement. Many times, we have no space for new acquisitions. My wife will ask me to remove some of my fancies so that there is room for the necessities. It is a good abundance.

There is an abundance of toys and gifts for everyone in the house during Christmas. There are always Christmas toys around my house year-round. This reminds me of my eldest sister's house because there is always an overflow of cooked food at her house. I remember driving fourteen hours from Atlanta to New York, hungry, wanting some of her well-cooked native food. The moment I opened her refrigerator, I was full. She had so much food in the refrigerator that it was overwhelming. There is always an abundance of food at my sister's house. She is always busy in the kitchen, cooking and trying to satisfy everyone.

Use the opportunity to pray for abundance and against lack in your life: "As I am experiencing this abundance, let it be so in every area of my life." Pray for the following and more:

- abundant respect
- abundant love
- abundant grace
- abundant mercy
- abundant favor
- abundant blessings
- spiritual abundance
- financial abundance

I was cleaning my liquidation store many years ago and realized that I had a lot of items that I was not aware of. I began to pray, "Lord, in the same way that I have all of these items that I was not aware of, let there be surplus in my life, in Jesus's name. Let there be an abundance of money in my accounts to the point that there is too much to count."

Let the blessings of God overtake you and be abundant in your life, in Jesus's name.

*H*oney Prayers

Honey is sweet and natural. Honey can be used to sweeten many things and is also a healthy alternative to sugar. You should not use honey if you are diabetic.

Honey is more expensive than white or brown sugar, but it is better for you. As you use your honey, pray that your life, marriage, family, and concerns will be as sweet as honey. Let your life be sweeter than honey in the name of Jesus.

Cheesecake Prayers

I love cheesecakes; they are a delight for me. I don't know what you like to eat that is sweet. Any time you are eating your favorite sweets, pray that the Lord will make your life even sweeter. Pray, "As sweet as this dessert is, so shall my marriage, health, and family be." You can use your best food or candy to pray this prayer. Do not use anything sour to pray this prayer. This prayer is all about sweetness. The more you pray, the sweeter your life will become, in the name of Jesus. The idea is to use anything and everything to pray.

Right-Food-Portion Prayers

Eat the right portion whenever you are eating. Choose quality over quantity when you are eating. Use your food as prayers. If you love to crack bones, pray with it. Make sure that you do not crack your teeth. Pray as you are enjoying your food that you will enjoy your life as much as you are enjoying the food: "As this food is right for me, give me what is right for me in my life, in Jesus's name. As I am enjoying this food and there are no bones to break my teeth, let my life be easy, in Jesus's name. Just as there are no bones, let there be no obstacles in my life, in Jesus's name. If there are bones, I crush them in the name of Jesus."

If you love to eat bones, pray, "Lord, if there are difficulties in my life as I am crushing these bones, let me crush them in Jesus's name. If there are enemies, Lord, give me the power to crush them in Jesus's name."

*F*lip-the-Coin-on-Food Prayers

Sometimes, you have no food to eat, just a little to eat, not enough to eat, you do not like the food you have to eat, or you have no other choice. Pray that your life will not be like this situation. Where you have no food to eat, let your life be the opposite. In a situation where you have little to eat, pray that God will provide enough for you and yours in the name of Jesus. Pray that, instead of eating what you do not like, you will always have enough in your home, in Jesus's name. Pray that sickness, lack, or poverty will not cause you to accept what you do not like, in Jesus's name.

*B*itter-Fruit Prayers

When you accidentally eat lemon, lime, bitter leaf, sour grapes, and sour oranges, pray that life will be the opposite of this bitter pill. In fact, pray that your life will not experience any bitterness, in Jesus's name. In 1 Chronicles 4:10, Jabez asked the Lord to "take this bitterness from me, take this pain from me, bless me, and enlarge my territory. Let Your right hand be upon my life to keep the enemy far away that I may not know sorrow again" (paraphrased). Immediately his prayer was answered.

Anytime you experience the opposite of your expectations (pain, suffering, struggling, a verdict that is not so good, a bad verdict, when you have to pay some money back, are evicted, guilty, divorced, going to prison, or fired), reverse it immediately in prayer. The power of life and death lies in the tongue. Whatever you bind on the earth is bound in heaven. Bind and refuse the verdict: "Father, if there is a verdict in the spiritual or natural realm that is not in my favor, I turn it around in Jesus's name."

Refuse any ugliness and every arrow sent your way. Words can be arrows, so refuse them and send them back to the sender in Jesus's name.

Expired-Food Prayers

Everything under the sun has an expiration date. I love my family, but they read every food label before buying to ensure that the items have not expired. Even our favorite movie or book will expire. There are also expiration dates on bottles and cans. Even products without an expiration stamp will expire. Expired food might mold, smell, or taste differently. In the same vein, evil, wickedness, problems, struggles, pain, and wilderness experiences must come to an end. Sicknesses, disappointments, and barrenness will all come to an end. The duration may vary from person to person. No matter the size of the book or the duration of the movie, they will all come to an end. As the book or movie ends, use it as a point of contact to pray for every struggle to cease in your life.

Cooking Prayers

I love well-sautéed food. Although I cannot cook, my Jamaican queen has a mastery of the kitchen. My wife goes all out at Thanksgiving with many palatable dishes on the table. As good as the food is for us, it can be cooked with the wrong intentions. This would all depend on who is holding the knife. My political-science professor died of poison when I was in college. The "love potion" that his wife put in his meal killed him.

Everything in life is a two-edged sword. Water can be a blessing or a curse. Your spouse can destroy you, make your life miserable, or be your pillar of strength or wealth. The tongue can tear down or build up. No matter how good the food is, it can turn sour. Pray for anyone who is cooking for you because your life is literally in their hands.

Pray against anyone cooking things that can bring harm to your family, health, business, home, or marriage. Pray that whatever they are cooking against you will be destroyed. The power of darkness is out there, working and cooking things to destroy you. The enemy has already peeped into your destiny and wants to destroy it before it begins. The enemy wants to delay or derail you if he cannot kill you. The enemy will hurl rumors at you to try to set you back. He will set obstacles and stumbling blocks before you to keep you from reaching your destiny. Do not just sit back and watch. Call out to the Holy Ghost's fire to destroy any pot of ingredients that are being used for cooking things against you, and you shall be free from the enemy's traps. Also, pray and destroy any evidence in the hands of the enemy against you.

Write Your Prayers and Thoughts Here

Nature Prayers

Nature gives us ample nudge into communion.

*S*unrise Prayers

The sun rises and sets every day. It rises in the east and sets in the west. As the sun is rising, use this time to pray. As the sun rises every day, people also rise every day from physical sleep. As it rises every day, you must rise the same way in the mighty name of Jesus. The sun must rise, so you too must arise. As the sun rises, your finances must rise, your children must rise, your anointing must rise, your family must rise, your health must rise, your business must rise, you must rise, in Jesus's name.

*D*ay and Night Prayers

God created day and night and made a covenant that night must always give way to daylight. The day must usher in the night, and that covenant cannot be broken. At about 5 a.m. every day, there is a clear sign that day is breaking. Night must disappear when the dawn of day breaks. The light must disappear when the sun goes down. Pray that as darkness is giving way to light, every darkness in your life must disappear. Pray that everything that makes your life experience darkness will disappear. Pray that whatever is bringing dark clouds into your life should disappear. As the day breaks each morning, breathe in the fresh air of a new day and pray for newness to come into your life in Jesus's name.

*U*mbrella *Prayers*

Umbrellas are meant to protect you from the heat of the scorching sun and rain and inclement weather. Pray as you are using the umbrella to protect you from the elements that God will shield you from any hazardous weather coming your way. Pray that God will shield you from sickness, lack, poverty, and shame. Pray that God will shield you with a pillar of cloud by day and a pillar of fire by night as He did for the Israelites in the wilderness. Pray that God will put a demarcation between you and the enemy forever, in Jesus's name.

*S*un *Prayers*

God created day and night. He created the moon to give light during the night and the sun to give light during the day. The sun is the most important source of energy. It is nearly a perfect sphere of hot plasma. The sun is the star at the center of the solar system that gives light and heat to all freely. I love sunshine, and that is why most people love summer. It illuminates; it gives light and warmth, and it drives away the blues. Pray as the sun shines brightly every day that God almighty will shine His love, grace, and mercy upon your life. Pray that God's best will shine upon you and yours. Pray that your life will also shine brightly and give light to all who come in your path. Pray to give warmth to as many as are in need. Pray to be a source of energy to many. Pray to be a supplier and a conduit of God's blessings. Pray to shine for all, to all, all the days of your life in Jesus's name.

Rain Prayers

According to *Merriam-Webster's Dictionary*, *rain* is water that falls from the clouds in small droplets.[1] Rain is very important, as it brings an increase, and without rain, the land would perish. Rain is necessary for the survival of many living organisms. Plants would wither away without rain. Rain is a gift from God. Whenever it rains, use it to pray: "Lord, as it is raining, let wealth fall on my home. Let wealth come from the east, west, north, and south. Let there be nonstop showers of blessings upon the lives of my spouse and children. Let goodness, long life, and prosperity rain in my life. Let there be a downpour of financial blessings in my life. Rain down blessings, O Lord, in Jesus's name. As it is raining outside, let it rain in my home. Let there also be the *latter rain* in my life. Amen."

Burning-Fire Prayers

Fires burn, destroy, and purify. When you see fire burning, it should be a reminder for you to pray. Pray

---

1 *Merriam-Webster.com Dictionary*, s.v. "rain," accessed May 26, 2022, www.merriam-webster.com/dictionary/rain.

that every evil in your life is burned and turned into ashes. Pray for ugliness and any evil intent in your life to be burned to ashes. Let the fire of God consume your enemies. Pray that the fire of the Holy Ghost will pursue those who are pursuing you and fight against those who are fighting you. Burn every evil plot and every messenger or agent of Satan. Let the fire of the Lord contend with them who contend with you. Let God destroy everything and anything that is trying to destroy you. May their paths be dark and slippery, in Jesus's name.

Write Your Prayers and Thoughts Here

CHAPTER 12

Entryway Prayers

*Open and closed entries and exits are living
necessities even on highways.*

Door Prayers

Doors can be described as portals and points used to go in and out of an enclosure. Doors are also boundary breakers. There are many things that go in and out that you cannot see with the naked eye. Therefore, it is important to see things through the spiritual eye. You cannot see the air you breathe or the contents of the air. Things that crawl or fly in and out of our home, not to mention what is moving around in the spiritual realm, are unseen. Demons and angels move in and out constantly, unbeknownst to us.

The prayer point is: "Father, put a guard on every portal, door, window, or any other mode of entrance in and out of my home. Guard my life, marriage, family, finances, and business. Guard me against unwarranted things, beings, or unauthorized persons who have access. Put holy angels on guard to drive away any evil and wickedness from my life. Drive out anything that can lead to pain, sorrow, confusion, depression, and failure, in the name of Jesus."

Put a barricade against any works of the enemy in your life, in Jesus's name.

Door-Opening Prayers

We open and close doors every day. Pray each time you open or close a door that the doors of good life, prosperity, good job, promotions, progress, good health, peace, victory, and joy will be opened to you. By the same token, when you close doors, pray that the Lord will close doors of disappointments, failures, negativity, court cases, lack, and poverty in your life.

Closed-Doors Prayers

A closed door is a barricade that hinders access in and out. A closed door can delay movement and send out a signal that you are not permitted to enter. A closed door can be the action of a hater. A closed door can be an act of wickedness caused by the enemy to stop your life from going in the right direction. A closed door could mean it is over.

If anyone closes a door in your face, instantaneously refuse and reject it. It is more than the action in the physical. If someone slams a door on you, it is saying that you are not wanted here, "so get out." Pray and reject it immediately. Pray that every closed door is opened and its effects are nullified in your life, in Jesus's name. When you are closing the door on your own, pray that every ugliness, failure, disappointment, or ugly experience may be noneffective in your life, in Jesus's name.

*L*ocks-and-Keys Prayers

We lock doors to prevent intruders or thieves from coming in to steal, kill, or destroy. We also lock doors at night to prevent the wicked ones, armed robbers, and night crawlers from invading our privacy. As you lock your doors, pray that in the physical and in the spiritual realm, the ones who come to kill, steal, and destroy will not gain access.

As you lock your doors when you go out, lock the doors against the enemy. As you lock your doors when you go to bed, lock them against all demons that rise at the midnight hour to take all that you have labored for. Lock the doors against intruders, lack, poverty, confusion, depression, and sickness, in Jesus's name. Lock the doors in prayer.

*D*ouble-Door Prayers

Doors are regular access points. When we were moving into a new house, our sofa would not fit through the door. We had to remove the door to give us access, but that did not work either. We were finally able to get the furniture in through a window. Removing windows to move furniture is a difficult task.

Oftentimes, a single door is not enough for all the blessings that God has for you. In most cases, double doors are needed. If that house had double doors, there would have been no reason to use a window. Double doors are wider, so it is easier to move furniture.

Double doors, double anointing, double promotions, but only one wife, please. There should be no double spouse. Anytime you open a double door or go through a double door, pray for double blessings upon your life, in Jesus's name.

*F*ences *Prayers*

Fences are barricades that prevent unauthorized persons from intruding into your territory. Fences are often put up to establish boundaries or property lines. A lot of people know neither how to set nor respect boundaries. It is important to set clear and visible boundaries. Pray that everyone and everything that is not invited into your life stays away in the name of Jesus. Put the barricades up against the enemy. Do not allow the accuser of the brethren to have anything against you. Build a fence of the Holy Ghost's fire around you and yours.

*W*indow-Blinds *Prayers*

Window blinds are meant to protect your privacy and direct rays from the sun. Pray for the Holy Spirit, in the same way, to shield you and your family from the enemy. Pray that your finances and your marriage are shielded by the blood of Jesus. Pray against all attacks from the enemy that will try to come against you. Pray that you are not exposed to the enemy either by your mouth or by your actions. Pray for God to cover you with the blood of Jesus so that the enemy will not see you.

As you get up in the morning and open your blinds to let the sunshine in, use this time to pray for God to open doors of prosperity and good health. When the sun goes down and you close your blinds, pray for God to open doors of prosperity and good health. Pray that every door of failure and disappointment will be closed in Jesus's name.

Write Your Prayers and Thoughts Here

Giving-and-Receiving Prayers

Your gift will make a way for you.

Gift-Giving Prayers

If you love to give gifts, keep giving them and let the gifts be good. Let not the gifts be given sparingly or grudgingly. The Word of God says it is better to give than to receive (Acts 20:35). Learn to give good gifts. Pray that as you are giving good gifts, heaven will also pour out many blessings that money cannot buy.

God knows what you really need and will give you the best. If you need a wife, husband, job, or good health, be specific when you ask. Do you remember making a Christmas list for Father Christmas? You were very detailed in your asking, and your parents saw fit to get you every item on the list. As you are making a list for your heavenly Father, through Christ Jesus, He will deliver. Take the details seriously, and it will come just the way you asked: "In this season, I am asking for a gift of good health." "I shall be very prosperous in Jesus's name."

Gift-Receiving Prayers

Receive gifts with joy and a heart of gratitude. We should not ever turn down a gift. When I came into ministry, it was my intention to give to the less privileged and not to receive from people. I was giving but was intentionally not receiving from anyone. One day, I was advised by one of the members that I was turning down my blessings. Receiving gifts and extending the joy of gratitude encourages the giver to always think of others more than of themselves.

Gifts are given freely from the heart. You did not earn or deserve it; the gift was a blessing. So, you should pray that your life will always be filled with gifts. People will come from the east, west, north, and south to bless you. Pray for more heavenly gifts to come your way. Pray that God will open His storeroom and shower His blessings upon you.

Remember to show gratitude for the gifts of long life, good health, abundance, and prosperity. Pray for gifts that can only come from God.

Money-Giving Prayers

It is good to help the less privileged. Ask the Holy Spirit to give you discernment as you are giving. Some people have wrong intentions and evil intent against those who reach out to help. God told me that the money and scriptures (letters) I was sending to my people were being used to tie me down. God will always let you know if you should give or not. You must pray before giving money to people. Cover the money with the blood of Jesus before you give it out. Pray that the money will be used for the intended purpose and then release the money with the Holy Ghost's fire.

When you pray before giving money, you are canceling and reversing the plan of the enemy. Any curse against you will be nullified. Any incantation, divination, or imagination will not prosper. No weapon formed against you will prosper (Isaiah 54:17). No, not one—in the name of Jesus.

Write Your Prayers and Thoughts Here

CHAPTER 14

Restoration Prayers

Restoration is the act of bringing something that existed back either by repairing or cleaning.

*F*loor-Covering Prayers

Beautiful well-finished oak wood, ceramic tiles, and carpeting are sometimes used to cover unfinished floors or to update outdated flooring. I build houses, and some homeowners do not want to be exposed to the details of the house construction or repairs. Pray that, as this carpet is covering the imperfections of the construction, the Holy Spirit covers any imperfection in your life. Pray to be covered from your enemies, sins, temptations, and strange eyes or legs in the name of Jesus: "Cover me from the track and radar of the enemy. Shield me with Your pillar of cloud by day and pillar of fire by night."

Pray also that God would cover your shame and disgrace and lead you to victory in the name of Jesus.

*N*ewness Prayers

I am not fond of old houses or old things; I love new things. I like new cars, new shining tires, the smell of a new car, the sounds of a new engine, and the fresh smell of new seats. New things give you the joy and satisfaction of admiring their beauty. Newness brings about a celebration from family and friends.

Anytime you buy something new, or something new is given to you, pray that your life will also experience newness. Pray that just as this new car is shining, the life of your spouse and children will also shine. Pray that as your life is shining, it will bring joy to you and everyone around you. Pray that the newness will give your family and you a breath of fresh air. Pray that the blessings of the Lord will make you rich and add no sorrow, in the name of Jesus.

*F*resh-Paint Prayers

When you buy a house, you want to make it look new by painting it. Painting gets rid of the old look and odors by giving it a fresh therapeutic look. You do not want to look at that old peeling paint or dirty wall. As you apply the new coat of paint, pray that everything that is old in your life will be covered with freshness. Pray that God will turn every struggle into progress, lack into plenty, and poverty into wealth. The old man must pass away; behold, the new one must come—so shall it be with you, in the name of Jesus.

Write Your Prayers and Thoughts Here

CHAPTER 15

Purity and Holiness Prayers

Come like little children.

Pups-and-Puppy Prayers

A puppy is a juvenile dog, while a *pup* refers to the baby of animals like seals and giraffes. Pups and puppies look beautiful, harmless, and innocent. Pray that your life will be beautiful, harmless, lovely, wonderful, hopeful, and full of vitality in Jesus's name.

Newborn-Baby Prayers

Newborn babies are beautiful, unique, special, innocent, adorable, and inviting. No one wants to harm a newborn baby except those who are twisted in their minds. Everyone wants to love and cherish a newborn. Pray that as this baby is fresh, new, unique, innocent, wonderful, and sweet, so will your life be. As no one in their right mind wants to harm a newborn, let no one think about harming you or your family, in the name of Jesus. Pray that as everyone wants to love and cherish the baby, so shall it be with you, in Jesus's name.

Write Your Prayers and Thoughts Here

CHAPTER 16

Technology-Usage Prayers

Use your tech tools and machines to form a prayer habit.

*C*ellphone *Prayers*

Cellphones used to be a new phenomenon but not anymore. When I was growing up, we had black-and-white televisions and digital-dial phones. When this invention came along, we thought it was cool. Next, we had car phones, which were big boxes screwed down in the car with the phone enclosed and an antenna to pull out when you needed to make a call.

This generation is so smart, creative, and innovative. We now have small palm-sized cellphones that cost more than a desktop computer. You can now speak to all and sundry at will from the convenience of your bathroom throne. Cellphones give you instant access to documents, phone numbers, and a wealth of information. Pray that as you use your cellphone to communicate at high speed, whatever is slow in your life will be fast and efficient. As you take on the sometimes-daunting task of learning to operate your cellphone, pray that whatever is hard in your life will become easy. Every desert ground shall become the garden of Eden in Jesus's name. Life must be sweeter, easier, and better in the name of Jesus.

*S*tatic-Noise *Prayers*

There are times we are on the phone and cannot hear our counterparts. There is so much static phone noise, especially on cellphones and during international calls. There are times we are in a dead zone, and there is no reception. Some people do not have any cellphone reception in their own homes; they must go outside to have a conversation. Static noise is a deal-breaker, obstacle, and hindrance, and sometimes, it stops your vision.

Pray that every static noise in your life, marriage, children's lives, and finances will be removed in the name of Jesus. You want to live a static-noise-free life. Your finances should not come to a stop. In fact, there should be a continuous flow of your finances in the name of Jesus. Your children should have no obstacles, in the name of Jesus. Every giant standing against you must vanish, in Jesus's name. Pray for a noise-free relationship with God; let it never be broken in the name of Jesus. There shall be no static noise but a direct link between you and God always, in Jesus's name.

Write Your Prayers and Thoughts Here

CHAPTER 17

Relaxation Prayers

*There is a time for everything: a time to work
and a time to rest.*

*L*aying-Down-to-Rest Prayers

It is God's design that we rest after a hard day's work. Lack of rest can lead to stress or illnesses. You can experience headaches, migraines, body aches, high blood pressure, and much more. You must get a good night's rest if you want to feel rejuvenated and ready to conquer the day. Pray as you lay down to sleep and rest that God will give you rest in your life, rest in your finances, and rest from trouble. Pray that God will give you the kind of rest that He gave to King Solomon in the Bible. Nothing missing, nothing broken. Let God give you that kind of rest, in Jesus's name. Rest in your marriage; rest from the children, bill collectors, court issues, wars, struggles, pain, troubles, fears, and doubts. Pray that the God of rest will grant you rest from all calamities, afflictions, and tribulations, in Jesus's name.

*L*istening-to-Music Prayers

Music is often called "food for the soul." As good food makes us feel satisfied and happy, so does music. My wife's love for music is above average. Music is sweet to the ears, melodious, unites people, sets the atmosphere, makes you dance, laugh, and it uplifts your spirit.

God also loves good music that is edifying and coming from true worshippers. Pray that your life will be so melodious that people will dance with joy just at the mention of your name. As you are dancing, people will rejoice and dance because of you. As you are listening and enjoying your favorite music, pray that God's voice and words will be so melodious to your ears that you will begin to dance, praise, and shout with joy because of His goodness.

Vacation Prayers

Vacation is the absence from a regular job for the purpose of recreation or rest. Vacations are meant for you to rest and rejuvenate. A vacation should be a change from your normal routine. This is the time to get your beauty rest, relax, get pampered, order room service, get a massage, eat good food, see a good Broadway show, and live stress-free. Personally, this is my type of vacation! I dread vacations where you are stuck in traffic for hours, mountain climbing, rabbit chasing, returning to the hotel late, and not getting sufficient rest. Vacations like that leave you wanting to take a vacation from the vacation. If you like this type of vacation, then, by all means, enjoy it.

As you are relaxing on your vacation, pray that your life will always be joyous, you will always be pampered and well attended to. Whatever you need shall be at your beck and call. Who says that you cannot or do not deserve a life like this? The Bible says,

These things I have written to you who believe in the name of the Son of God, that you may know that you have eternal life, and that you may continue to believe in the name of the Son of God. Now this is the confidence that we have in Him, that if we ask anything according to His will, He hears us.

1 John 5:13–14

There are people who have maids and drivers; why not? Ask, and it shall be given to you (Matthew 7:7).

Reading and Movies Prayers

Some of us love to read, while others enjoy watching movies. Reading is recommended for all school-aged children and for those who need to get by in this world. We should develop a culture of reading and still watch a good movie when we can. It is recommended that we watch educational and entertaining movies rather than horror movies. Laughter is good medicine, and horror movies can open doors to demonic attacks.

As you are enjoying your favorite movie or reading your favorite book, pray that God will bring laughter and joy into your life, in the name of Jesus.

I feel so disappointed when a good movie or a good book comes to an end, but they must end. As the book or movie ends, use this as a point of contact to pray for every struggle to cease in your life.

Write Your Prayers and Thoughts Here

Part B.

Must Know

There are rules of engagement. A knowledge of why, when, and how victory comes.
These sections deal with what we should know about some very important spiritual matters.

Introduction

One must understand the rules of engagement to ensure victory in war. According to *Britannica, rules of engagement* are "part of a general recognition that procedures and standards are essential to the conduct and effectiveness of civilized warfare."[2]

Believers are constantly in spiritual warfare. Trouble comes looking for you even when you do not want to war. It is, therefore, imperative for you to understand how to fight to win. The rules of engagement must be a way of life because the battle is constant. Rules of engagement are to be used not only to fight back but also to teach you how to pursue instead of being pursued.

The spiritual battle is more real than the physical. The spiritual battle is deadlier, well calculated, and more powerful and has lasting and devastating effects on the victim. When you are running for your life, you must know the following rules of engagement.

2 *Encyclopaedia Britannica*, editors of *Encyclopaedia*, s.v. "rules of engagement," November 23, 2016, www.britannica.com/topic/rules-of-engagement-military-directives.

Spoken Words

Death and life are in the power of the tongue.

Proverbs 18:21

Spoken Words

There is tremendous power in spoken words. Do not ever underestimate the power of words. Words that are not used to bless others can harm them. Spoken words are not meaningless words. The spiritual world takes every word seriously. Jesus stated in Matthew 12:36, "But I say to you that for every idle word men may speak, they will give account of it in the day of judgment." Use words right, and they will move mountains. In the same way, spoken words against you can be very destructive.

The apostle James said in his writings in James 3:6, "And the tongue is a fire, a world of iniquity. The tongue is so set among our members that it defiles the whole body and sets on fire, the course of nature, and it is set on fire by hell." Hell uses spoken words to destroy. These words are called "incantations," "divination," "enchantments," "spells," and "invocations."

An *incantation, spell,* or *charm* is a magical formula intended to trigger a magical effect on a person or object. The formula can be spoken, sung, or chanted. An incantation can also be performed during ceremonial rituals or prayers. Wizards, witches, and fairies perform magic and incantations.

Enchantments are charms or spells. Being enchanted is a state of being under a spell or under magic. It is a world of mystery. It is used to influence and bewitch by the power of the spoken word.

Divination is used to gain insight into your life. An act of seeking knowledge of the future. The enemy sees your good bright future and will make every attempt to abort it. You may not necessarily know and understand the plans that God has for you, but the enemy does. The knowledge of your bright future motivates them into action against you. Their only purpose is to delay, stop, or harm you.

You must always pray against anyone who is trying to cause a delay in your life and finances. Pray against them trying to stop you from getting to your glorious destination.

Write Your Prayers and Thoughts Here

CHAPTER 18

Altars

Godly Altars

Satanic Altars

Altars are communion channels within the spiritual world. To live an abundant life, satanic altars, strongholds, chains, and curses must be broken and replaced with godly altars.

Altars

An altar is a place of spiritual sacrifice, a place of contact with the spiritual world, and a place of communion with God. Altars can also be used as an entry point of spirits into the world, a place where you activate covenants, and a launching pad for spiritual attacks. Altars can speak on your behalf and can also control your destiny. Altars can be crafting stations designed to make lives miserable. I prophesy against all satanic altars working against you and against the purpose of God in your life, in Jesus's name.

Godly Altars

Altars of God are sacred worship places that are erected using the precious blood of our Lord and Savior, Jesus Christ. No other blood is needed. His blood is good enough. His blood is for all who believe, and it is everlasting. His blood was shed once for the remission of sins for all mankind.

An altar is a physical place of prayer to commune with God and for spiritually communing in your mind. Every believer should have a place of communion or altar.

*S*atanic Altars

Satanic altars are places where sacrifices are offered to Satan and demons. This normally involves shedding both human and animal blood. Satanic altars cause limitations or hindrances. These altars are made potent by a combination of sacrifices and spoken words. The spiritual world operates in blood, hence the ultimate blood sacrifice of the Lamb of God.

The blood on satanic altars is always crying out. God told Cain that the blood of his brother was crying out to God. It is a place of spiritual exchange of glories and destinies. It is a melting point of divinity. I heard about a young lady whose brains were exchanged for stones. She was sent home from the university for academic failure. Previously, she was at the top of her class. Therefore, we cannot tell everyone about our progress. Achieve it first and broadcast it later.

A satanic altar is a place of spiritual fellowship for demonic spirits and demonic agents. It is like the altar of God except for the meaning and intended purposes. It is a place where satanic covenants or spiritual contracts are made and sealed. This is done whether those concerned are aware or not. As children of God, we should enter into covenant only with the blood of Jesus

Like a marriage covenant, all covenants have spiritual consequences. When I was growing up, many young ladies and men went into blood covenants, vowing never to leave each other. These covenants are satanic with grave spiritual consequences if the conditions of the covenants are not kept.

Satanic altars are seats of power. They are places where satanic warlords go to battle against God's people. Satanic altars are places of evil and spiritual transactions. Therefore, we must always pray. Satanic altars are places of spiritual monitoring. They set mirrors to see what you are doing. You can never be successful if you are satanically monitored. Pray against every altar erected against you. Pray that every altar where your name is mentioned will be destroyed in the name of Jesus and that everything that is not of God may be cut down with a Holy Ghost's machete. Pray for the Holy Ghost to blind every eye that is satanically monitoring you.

Satanic altars are also places of spiritual communication, reinforcement, and evaluation of satanic activities. They create unnecessary limitations and boundaries for people. They restrict our abilities and dictate how far we can go.

The book of Lamentations 3:37 reads, "Who is he who speaks, and it comes to pass when the Lord has not commanded it?" We should always pray, rebuke, and send back to the sender every arrow sent at us. Every incantation, enchantment, spell, and divination must be brought to naught. Satanic altars are there to oppose God and His grace in your life, delay God's plan for your life, cause unresolvable problems, and prolong afflictions. They exist to stop your progress, kill, steal, and destroy. You must be proactive and pray always.

You, too, can raise your altar. You can raise a godly altar where you can go and pray. Some call it their "prayer closet," "prayer corner," "war room," or a place where you can go and commune with your Maker.

Pulling Down Altars

It is important to pull down ungodly altars so that they do not stand against you. Only the power of Jesus can pull down satanic altars. Human knowledge and efforts cannot pull down ungodly altars. Zechariah 4:6c (NLT) reads, "It's not by force [...], but by my Spirit, says the LORD of Heaven's Armies."

You must be born again and must renounce all covenants with the devil, maintain a godly life, and understand that the Word of God is the only standard for believers. You must raise another altar if you want to stop satanic altars. It doesn't have to be a physical altar. It could be increasing your prayer life or setting up a physical altar where you pray daily and plead the blood of Jesus. The spiritual realm always engages blood when establishing altars. You have the blood of Jesus as a child of God.

Write Your Prayers and Thoughts Here

CHAPTER 19

Prayer Praise

Praise your way through.

*P*etition Prayers

A *petition*, according to dictionary.com, is "a request made for something desired."[3] We are always asking. Every day, every morning, every night, every time we pray, we are asking for one thing or the other. It sounds selfish: always praying for self, always asking for something.

We do not stop to ask God what He wants. These prayers are all about "me," "myself," and "I": "God, bless me," "God, provide for me," "God, protect me," "God, guide me," "God, bless my children," and "God, bless my wife [or husband]." "God, give us a new car," "God, give us a new house," "God, destroy my enemies."

There is nothing wrong with these prayers; it is important to pray for oneself. There comes a time when it becomes redundant and monotonous to ask for the same things over and over again. It begins to sound like a broken record and reveals selfish intentions.

*I*ntercession or Intercessory Prayers

Intercession prayer is the act of praying on behalf of others as the Holy Spirit gives you revelation. Pray for the needs of others, for lost souls, pray against the

---

3 Dictionary.com, LLC, s.v. "petition," accessed May 26, 2022, www.dictionary.com/browse/petitioned.

powers of darkness, pray for the nation and the leaders, and pray selflessly. Pray in an unknown tongue as the Spirit gives utterance, for it is a mystery that confuses the enemy. Praying for things and people who you know or don't know, just doing the will of the Father. Daniel had to pray for the whole country. King Solomon was also tasked to pray for his country and to pray for the sins of his forefathers and the people. Jesus prayed for believers now and believers to come in John 17.

*P*rayer Praise

Prayer praise is faith in action. For without faith, it is impossible to please the Father. It is calling those things that be not as if they are. It is thanking God for the manifestation, and yet you have not seen it in the natural. It is believing that God heard your prayers and has answered them. It can be in both intercessory prayers and the "I want" prayers. When you have satisfactorily prayed for someone or something, praise God for it. At this point, it is no longer redundant or mere words. It is no longer just wind. It becomes a faith walk. Whatever you bind on the earth is bound in heaven. Whatever you loose on the earth is loosed in heaven.

Examples of praise prayer include:

"I praise You, God, for my spouse." Maybe your spouse is not acting right, but you are giving thanks.

"I thank You, God, for my children." Maybe you don't even have children yet, or they are not on the right path, but you are thanking God for them.

"I thank You for the promotion." Maybe it is not your turn to be promoted, and instead, that's your subordinate's.

"I thank You, God, for my new vehicle"—and you don't have a new vehicle yet.

"I thank You for enlarging my territory."

"I thank You for the increase."

Most of the time, only you and God truly know what you are thanking Him for. "I thank God for my children." What exactly are you thanking God for? What is it that you need for your children? Do you want the best for them? Do you want them to do well in school, in life, or to be obedient? It becomes a secret weapon that the enemy has no clue what you are really saying.

God knows exactly the intentions of your heart. The Holy Spirit, who knows all things, sees all things, understands all things, will present your request before His Majesty, in Jesus's name.

Prayer praise makes praying easy. It is not the eloquence of words; it is the simplicity and the sincerity of a grateful heart. It moves the heart of God to action unless your hands are stained. If your hands are stained, your praise becomes an abomination. Repent before you approach the throne of grace if you want your praise to be accepted.

I encourage you to use prayer praise more than any other kind of prayer. After you have petitioned or prayed for others, end your prayer sessions with prayer praising and thanking God for answering prayers. The God of all flesh will answer you in due season.

Write Your Prayers and Thoughts Here

CHAPTER 20

Mirroring

There are mirrors that are used to monitor your progress. You must shatter any mirror used against you.

*M*onitoring Mirrors/Agents

According to Pastor Martin (2016), "evil spiritual monitoring" is

> when a person [...] who has spiritual knowl-
> edge and the eyes of the spirit puts another
> person under constant watch or monitoring
> for evil intent. All because they do not want
> the glory of God upon that person. [4]

They put their subject in a mirrorlike object so that they can see your every move. This enables them to stop your progress. Monitoring objects include but are not limited to mirrors, brooms, tarot cards, crystal balls, voodoo, waterpots, basins, human agents, snakes, animals, and more. There is no distance in the spiritual realm, and anyone with spiritual eyes can investigate another person's life and see what's going on. Once this is done, they set traps, snares, cast spells, incantations, and divinations against their subject to cause harm, derail, stop progressive upward movement, and frustrate destinies.

In the mirror, a representation of your past, present, and future can culminate together in one place.

---

4 Pastor Martin, "Evil spiritual monitoring," Melchizedek Church of God, October 11, 2016, www.mcgonline.net/evil-spiritual-monitoring.

This gives them the opportunity to know how to achieve their evil objectives against you. The sole purpose is to make God out to be a liar in your life. The opportunity to monitor one's life is caused by the lack of prayer life and the presence of sin, iniquity, spiritual defilement, and bloodguiltiness.

Ecclesiastes 10:8b (KJV) says, "Whoso breaketh an hedge, a serpent shall bite him." Live a God-fearing life and shatter every monitoring mirror. Destroy every monitoring agent and object in your life through a prayer lifestyle. God has given you the power to tread upon serpents and scorpions, and they shall by no means hurt you. He has given you power over the enemy, and nothing shall hurt you. These are human agents, appearing and disappearing agents assigned to monitor your progress and to prevent the glory of God over your life. There are strange eyes watching you and strange legs following you. They are all in a bid to frustrate your life and make God a liar in your life. God is not a man that He should lie or a son of man that He should repent. As He promised, will He not do it?

These are some of the signs of evil monitoring: eating in dreams, cobwebs on your face in unexpected places, sex in dreams, being chased in your dream, miscarriages caused by evil spirits. Sudden rodent infestations, nightmares, making money in dreams, snakes watching you or attacking in dreams, and more. An attack is imminent; an invasion is about to take place. This is a sign that they are about to run you over. You must go into warfare prayers, not pretty or casual prayers. This is serious; this is a time when you must fight back if you do not want to be defeated.

When I pray, I pray against strange legs and strange eyes. I take a Holy Ghost's machete, cut off strange legs, and pour Holy Ghost's acid on strange eyes to blind them. I release Holy Ghost's fire to burn to ashes every monitoring agent and object.

Shatter every mirror and destroy whatever they are using against you. Please know that there are no coincidences in life. When something happens to you, try to handle it spiritually first.

Write Your Prayers and Thoughts Here

Part C.

Midnight Exchange

CHAPTER 21

Midnight Exchange

Time for war: the enemy is not bowing out easily. So, an outstretched hand of God is needed. Go into battle and fight for what you believe. As you fight in the natural, it is happening in the spiritual realm.

The enemy is like a roaring lion seeking whom he may devour (1 Peter 5:8). The enemy comes to kill, steal, and destroy. He is tireless in his pursuit to destroy your peace and steal your joy. He will make your life miserable and reduce you to an unhappy and senseless individual if you let him. The enemy will make you wallow in the valley of hopelessness and helplessness if you don't stop him. His hope is that you will wallow with the swine, be judged as unwise, foolish, or a nobody and become a failure.

The Word of God admonishes us in James 4:7 to "resist the devil and he will flee." Prayer changes things, and praise brings redemption. Understand that Jesus came to destroy the works of the devil. Not only did He come to make Satan's efforts ineffective but to give us abundant life. It is pertinent, therefore, to engage in spiritual warfare to put an end to the ways of the lawless one, whose sole objective is to make you suffer. The result of that would be to derail you until you turn your back on your Lord and Savior, Jesus Christ. The evil one will not succeed over our lives, in Jesus's name, amen.

Midnight

The midnight hour is the time when evil demons are let loose. This is the time when the enemy comes to kill, steal, and destroy. The demons are busy coming up with the next attack on your life while you are sleeping. All that is wicked comes out during the midnight hour. When you are asleep, demons are awake. While you cannot see them, they grope around as if it is daytime. The enemy is trained to hunt and hurt you during the midnight hour.

Darkness cannot stand light. There are some creatures that cannot come out during the day because the light affects them. It is very destructive to them. They can only come out at midnight.

There are some demons that specialize in making your life miserable at midnight. Prayer is essential during this time of night.

Friends can hurt you in darkness, and you will not be aware of it. They will laugh with you during the day and harm you at night. They will sympathize with you in public, and behind your back, they are your worst nightmare. Pray that God will open your eyes to the various spirits around you. Pray for the spirit of discernment to be able to differentiate a friend from an enemy. Everyone who rolls out the "red carpet" for you is not necessarily a friend. Beware of "red carpets." (For more information on this, please see our book *Snakes in the Holy Ghost Uniform*, which will be available in the fall of 2022.)

Have you ever noticed that most clubs open at night? I personally don't know one club that is open during the day. I know an entire tribe that will not attend a function until very late. I was once invited to a function that was to start at 8:00 p.m. I arrived at 9:00 p.m., thinking that I was very late. I noticed that the only people who were there when I came were the organizers. I asked one of them if the function was still being held. The organizer said yes. As I sat there, I noticed that people started arriving close to the midnight hour. They started to arrive in droves as if they were waiting somewhere and had just been released. The person who invited me informed me that this was the norm. He told me that they normally showed up by midnight.

I begin to think about how criminals, the occult, witchcraft, and covens prosper in darkness and midnight. The book of John 3:19–21 says,

> And this is the condemnation, that the light has come into the world, and men loved darkness rather than light because their deeds were evil. For everyone practicing evil hates the light and does not come to the light, lest his deeds should be exposed. But he who does the truth comes to the light, that his deeds may be clearly seen, that they have been done in God.

A believer, a God-fearing being, has no business running around in the night unless they are trying to stop the wicked. Believers who are spiritually attuned to how the enemy operates will get up at midnight to pray. Praying at midnight can counterattack the ways of the wicked one. The mystery of the night is deep and cannot be fully understood. As believers, we have to stay vigilant and pray during the midnight hour.

The Midnight Exchange

In 1 Kings 3, there were two prostitutes who gave birth at the same time. These women shared one bed with the two newborn infants. One of the mothers mistakenly rolled over and killed her baby. At midnight, she got up and exchanged her dead baby for the other woman's living baby.

Evil is perpetrated at midnight when it is dark and no one is watching. When you can hide and think that no one is looking. Evil persons feel empowered because they think that no one will ever know or stop them.

This is what the enemy does. At midnight, he exchanges your good health for sickness. At midnight, he takes the life of your baby and exchanges it for a dead baby. The enemy comes to change your destiny, afflict you, take your possessions, take your spouse, take your wealth, and exchange it for poverty. The enemy comes to take your happy home and exchange it for a broken home. The enemy will turn your well-behaved children against you if you give him a chance. The enemy attacks at midnight. Therefore, you must put on the whole armor of God so that you may be able to stand against the wiles of the devil.

What happens when you are awake is what has happened at midnight. From midnight to 3 a.m. is a crucial time for spiritual warfare.

*N*eed for Warfare

The Oxford dictionary defines warfare as "engagement in or the activities involved in war or conflict."[5] It is obvious that we are in a constant battle for our lives. It is, therefore, important to know the rules of engagement. The rules of engagement teach us how to be victorious.

It may look as if you are the one making the wrong choices, foolish moves, or saying the wrong things, but it is the spirit of manipulation at work. I used to hear voices in my head that would tell me to go and kill myself. Sometimes the voices would say, "You can't make it; you are a failure," "Slap your wife," You are the man; what you say goes." Had I acted on these taunting voices, there would have been grave consequences.

---

5 Lexico.com, s.v. "warfare," accessed May 26, 2022, www.lexico.com/definition/warfare.

To fight and overcome that which is unseen, we must understand the kind of battle that we need to prepare for. Second Corinthians 10:3–5 reads,

> For the weapons of our warfare are not carnal but mighty in God for the pulling down strongholds, casting down arguments and every high thing that exalts itself against the knowledge of God, bringing every thought into captivity to the obedience of Christ and being ready to punish all disobedience when your obedience is complete.

It literally means that this battle or this warfare is not physical; it's not the kind that you use your fist or weapons to fight. This is not a flesh-and-blood war; you are not fighting humans.

This is a spiritual fight that you are fighting. The enemy is an expert in this spiritual game. He knows you better than you know yourself. He understands who you are, what language you speak, your culture, your background, your weaknesses, and what makes you angry. The enemy can easily press your buttons and stand back and watch you fall. How then can you fight this battle to win? Therefore, you must know yourself, the enemy, and how to overcome him. Having done it all, stand!

Who Is the Enemy?

I heard a story of a new convert in Sunday school. The new convert raised his hand to ask a question, "I have been hearing of 'the enemy,' 'the enemy,' 'the enemy.' Who is 'the enemy'?" Everyone laughed, but he asked a very important question. *Who is the enemy?*

Satan, the devil, the lawless one, the dragon, the antichrist, the wicked one, the father of all lies, the one who fights against God, and the accuser of the brethren. For the most part, we do not understand his ways, how he thinks, why he comes against us, how he comes against us, when he comes against us, when he moves, or the kinds of weapons he deploys. Because we do not know, we must, therefore, engage the services of one who knows. We should seek help by engaging the one who is familiar with the tactics of the enemy. There is only one who has defeated the enemy, and that being is not flesh and blood.

The one who has defeated the enemy, the dark one, is the light, the true light, the anointed one.

It takes special equipment to defeat darkness. The only one who can defeat him possesses all power in heaven and earth and underneath the earth. This battle can only be fought and won by the one who has defeated Satan. The finished work on the cross defeated darkness. This access that was given to us through grace and mercy can be used against the enemy if you believe in the only begotten Son of God, the true light, a gift to mankind. There is, therefore, a great need to be on Jesus's side if you want to win. Apart from believing in Him, you must walk right, live in peace, love, gentility, meekness, long-suffering, obedience, and prayer. By so doing, you are turning on the light, and darkness must dissipate.

Ephesians 6:12–13 says it very loudly,

> We do not wrestle against flesh and blood, but against principalities, against powers, against the rulers of the darkness of this age, against spiritual hosts of wickedness in the heavenly places. Therefore, take up the whole armor of God that you may be able to withstand in the evil day, and having done all, to stand.

We must pray to pull down these strongholds, principalities, and wickedness in high places. We must pray to engage spiritual warriors, led by the captain of the army of the Lord, to fight for us. I encourage you to form and keep a prayer habit if you want to win and not struggle. First Peter 5:8 says, "Be sober, be vigilant, because your adversary the devil walks about like a roaring lion, seeking whom he may devour."

*S*top Them

Prayer is the weapon of warfare. It is an invitation to the archangel and our redeemer to arise on our behalf. Luke 6:12 encourages us to pray all night, and every association of wickedness gathered against us will be scattered because of our tenacity. Pray. If you cannot pray all night, still get up and pray. Your breakthrough is nonnegotiable. Prayer opens doors for your life, opens doors of progress, good health, harmonious living, and upward mobility.

They want to stop or derail you, so you must act first and swiftly; you must stop them. You must be on the offensive. Pursue those who are pursuing you, fight against those who are fighting against you, trouble those who trouble you, destroy those who are trying to destroy you, torment your tormentors.

You cannot sleep all the time. Wake up at midnight and fight. Fight for what you believe; fight for what you care about. Make praying your lifestyle so that you can enjoy perpetual peace, prosperity, good success, good health, and a life of bliss.

Spiritual wickedness in high places, rulers of darkness, dream manipulators, principalities, and powers are programmed for increased activity at midnight. They operate efficiently under cover of darkness. It is better to prevent them from planting evil in your garden than to look for a solution after the deed is done. Power has been given to you through Jesus Christ. Just pray and do a midnight exchange as often as you can. Send those arrows back to the sender. Stand on your guard to quench the fiery darts of the wicked.

*M*ystery of Speaking in Tongues

Like midnight exchange, speaking in tongues is a weapon that we should always use. Jeff M. Daniel emphasized the benefits of 1 Corinthians 14:2, "For he who speaks in tongues does not speak to men but to God, for no one understands him; however, in the spirit he speaks mysteries." Daniel says speaking in tongues is a mystery. If speaking in tongues is properly understood, believed, and applied, it can turn anyone's life into a glorious mystery. According to Daniel, "God's heavenly language, which is called *speaking in tongues*, shuts your mouth from talking like a human being to thinking and acting like the spiritual being that you actually are."[6] Speaking in tongues will give you access to the deep things of God.

Satan is the prince of the air, so speaking in tongues is speaking into the air to diffuse and destroy all satanic operations against your life and destiny.

---

6 "About the author," *Mystery of Speaking in Tongues,* Google Books, accessed May 26, 2022, www.books.google.com/books/about/Mystery_of_Speaking_in_Tongues.html?id=kdHvjgEACAAJ.

The Enemy Is Not Playing with You

Satan is an entity in the Abrahamic religion that seduces humans into sin or falsehood (*Britannica*, 2022). Responding to *Britannica's* definition: Satan, the devil, is not just in Abrahamic religion but is still referred to as the seducer and accuser of mankind today. He lures people into sin and falsehood. It is as relevant a concern today as it was decades ago. He was the enemy then and is still the enemy today. Satan is not only a seducer of humans but a lawless one who ravages, kills, steals, and destroys lives. He causes havoc minute by minute across villages, cities, counties, parishes, regions, states, and nations.

Satan is like a chameleon. He is always changing his tactics and methods of attack on believers. In fact, he masquerades as an angel of light. It is his job to whittle down our faith in Christ Jesus to create doubt and fear. It is his job to make serving Christ difficult. He introduces hardships for you to give up your mission of being a true believer. It is his job to destabilize marriages and homes so that the dysfunction created can lead to a drastic reduction in the number of children trusting and believing in God. If they cannot trust their father to be there for them, how will they trust God, who they have not seen?

The enemy does not deserve any credit, but he is very crafty and smart; he is good at his job. Now God must do extra work to get us to live His promise. John 10:10 says, "The thief does not come except to steal, and to kill, and to destroy. I have come that they may have life, and that they may have it more abundantly." While God is doing the fighting and putting an end to the lawlessness created by the enemy, you must tell God what you want and how you want it. So, we must pray always.

Write Your Prayers and Thoughts Here

Generational Curses

[...] the iniquity of the fathers upon the children to the third and fourth generations of those who hate Me.

Exodus 20:5b

Generational Curses

Blessings or curses are words spoken with some sort of spiritual power and authority. Whether good or bad, this sets in motion something that can go on from generation to generation. According to Makashinyi (2019), a *generational curse* describes the cumulative effect on a person of things that their ancestors did, believed, or practiced in the past and a consequence of an ancestor's actions, beliefs, and sins being passed down.[7]

The Bible in Exodus 20:5b spoke about generational curses thus, "For I, the LORD your God, am a jealous God, visiting the iniquity of the fathers upon the children to the third and fourth generations."

Just in case I was missing something, the same thought was emphasized in Exodus 34:7b, "By no means clearing the guilty, visiting the iniquity of the fathers upon the children and the children's children to the third and the fourth generation." Lamentations 5:7 reopened in the book of Ezekiel 18:2b, "The fathers have eaten sour grapes, and the children's teeth are set on edge." The actions and beliefs of the fathers have repercussions on the children, even in the third and fourth generations.

Why is this information of any relevance to prayer?

---

7 Makashinyi, The Gospel Coalition (2019), www.africa.thegospelcoalition.org/article/truth-behind-generational-curses.

It is crucial to know the root cause of a problem if you are going to deal with it adequately. A list of such curses includes but is not limited to misfortunes, afflictions, disasters, damnations, tribulations, failures without reasons, poverty, lack, repeated cycles of the same thing, a continuous pattern of struggle, continued defeat, and more. When these things keep happening, you know it is a generational curse. If generational curses are not broken, they will destroy your life and could affect you and your lineage.

Examples of such curses include:

- In some families, the women do not stay in marriages. It is a curse that must be broken.
- In some families, the men are not successful; they are always failing. It is not a coincidence.
- In America, an African American had never become president until Obama broke the cycle, and now Kamala Harris, the first Black, Asian American female, is to be vice president.
- Some people are just plagued with poverty. No matter what they do, they are always poor.
- Some persons are tormented with nightmares. They cannot even sleep peacefully in their own homes. There is always something to keep them awake.

- Some persons are underachievers. They never rise past an invisible boundary.
- In the '90s in New York, there were a lot of people in the Bronx who went after welfare checks and free housing. They gave birth to a lot of children because they felt this would help them to get more money from the government. They did not realize that this was not normal behavior. My assistant is a New Yorker who turned down free low-income housing as a way of breaking that generational curse over her family. She later bought her own house and is happily married, living a curse-free life.
- Some people have a curse of never being satisfied financially or sexually. They always want another husband or wife. They always want something new, but this is not excitement; it is a curse.
- Some are cursed with alcoholism and drug abuse. They drink or do drugs till they die.
- Some persons are cursed with an untimely death.
- Some are cursed with the spirit of suicide.

It is imperative to know these abnormalities so that you can overcome them. We already know that we can only be an overcomer by the blood of the Lamb and the word of our testimony.

Curses Have Causes

Curses and problems have roots. You must go to the root of the problem if you are going to solve it. Stop treating the symptom and uproot it. It is good to find out who your father is and who your grandparents were. Find out their deeds. Were they loving, or were they wicked to others? The answers will give you an idea behind certain mishaps in your life.

Spoken words have power, so stop speaking negatively into your children's lives:

1. "You are stupid."
2. "You will amount to nothing."
3. "You are a goat."
4. "You are dumb."
5. "You can never do anything right."
6. "You are just like your daddy."

Speak life instead of curses. Curses affect the lives of the second and even the fourth generation. Wives, when you speak negatively to your husband, you are placing a curse on yourself and your children and your children's children.

Sin is also a major cause of curses. Sexual sins can cause curses on your life. If you slept with somebody's wife, the curse might be everybody will sleep with your wife. That is what happened to King David. Friends and relatives slept with David's concubines.

Sin will bring a curse on you, your children, and your children's children.

Dabbling in witchcraft, rebellion, murder, not paying tithes, touching God's anointed, and turning your back on the poor can bring a curse on you and your family. Curses block your blessings and lead to:

- poverty
- struggling
- brokenness
- unfruitfulness
- sickness
- setbacks
- failure
- death

The good news is that Christ has redeemed us from the curse of the law. So, generational curses can be broken in Jesus's name.

Breaking Generational Curses

Curses are like umbrellas that prevent your blessings from reaching you. If generational curses are not broken, certain prayers will go unanswered, and pain and suffering will continue. We must go to the root of the problem to break a generational curse. The blood of Jesus must be applied to break curses. You must reverse every negative word that has been spoken over your life. You must reject negative incantations, enchantments, and divinations spoken against you and your forefathers that have affected you or are still affecting you.

Some of the major curses are included in Deuteronomy 27:15–26.

> Cursed is the one who makes a carved or molded image, an abomination to the LORD [...] Cursed is the one who treats his father or his mother with contempt [...] Cursed is the one who moves his neighbor's landmark [...] Cursed is the one who makes the blind to wander off the road [...] Cursed is the one who perverts the justice due the stranger, the fatherless and widow. [...] Cursed is the one who lies with his father's wife because he has uncovered his father's bed. [...] Cursed is the one who lies with any kind of animal. [...] Cursed is the one who lies with his sister, the daughter of his father or the daughter of his mother. [...] Cursed is the one who lies with his mother-in-law [...] Cursed is the one who

attacks his neighbor secretly. [...] Cursed is the one who takes a bribe to slay an innocent person. [...] Cursed is the one who does not confirm all the words of this law by observing them.

King David was a victim of curses. David slept with Beersheba, Uriah's wife, and then killed Uriah. Ammon, David's son, slept with his sister Tamer. Absalom, David's son, killed Ammon and went on self-exile. He returned to overthrow his father, David, and planned to kill him. Absalom was killed in the process.

They are not coincidental happenings. Break every generational curse.

Write Your Prayers and Thoughts Here

CHAPTER 23

Divine Exchange

Greater love has no one than this, than to lay down one's life for his friends.

John 15:13

Divine Exchange

We need a divine exchange to change some things and eradicate curses in our lives. Jesus Christ, the only begotten Son of God, who became flesh and dwelt among men, who knew no sin, became sin for the sake of mankind. He was guiltless but became guilty, a judge—but became the judged and weak for our sake that we might be strong. The healer became the wounded; He became the exchanged item on the exchange table. Jesus became cursed so that we could be free. The divine exchange is summarized in one word, "salvation." If you believe in your heart and confess with your mouth that Jesus died and rose from the grave, you are saved from any curse.

Some examples of warfare prayers:

1. Matthew 27:5: pray that God will expose your enemies who ate, danced, and walked with you but want to betray you. Pray for God to expose and deal with your "frenemies."
2. Mark 16:4: pray that any stone rolled to block your destiny, future, and finances is rolled away in Jesus's name.
3. First Kings 14:9–11: pray that they shall be cursed with the Jeroboam curse and that vultures will eat the bodies of the dead. None of them will be buried, for their bodies will not be found.

4. Matthew 27:50: Jesus cried with a loud voice and died. Pray that every problem in your life must die. Every enemy of your progress must die. Shout aloud as Jesus did, "It is finished," and let them die in Jesus's name.
5. Second Samuel 9:1: pray for men to favor you.
6. Luke 4:13: pray for every evil in your life to expire.
7. Psalm 4:2: pray that God removes anyone who tries to turn your glory into shame.

The Lord Is in Need of You

In Luke 19:30–31, Jesus called two of his disciples and sent them, saying,

> Go into the village opposite you, where as you enter you will find a colt tied, on which no one has ever sat. Loose it and bring it here. And if anyone asks you, "Why are you loosing it?" Thus, you shall say to him, "Because the Lord has need of it."

God said to Moses in Exodus 9:1, "Go in to Pharaoh and tell him, 'Thus, says the LORD God of the Hebrews: "Let My people go, that they may serve Me."'"

Lazarus in John 11 was raised by Jesus Christ from the dead. He came out, bound from head to toe, and in

John 11:44, Jesus commanded them to lose him and let him go.

Satan holds God's people in bondage. It is imperative to be free. You cannot function well if you are bound.

The enemy holds people down spiritually, financially, matrimonially, mentally, and sexually. The enemy can make lives difficult and uneasy. You must command them to loose you in your destiny so you can enjoy your life. Many persons are unaware that they are tied down in different ways. Your breakthrough is for a purpose, your millions are not just for you, your freedom is for a reason, your calling is not for you to shine, and your wealth is not to be hidden in a bank account so you can boast of how much you have.

Jesus said to them, "The Lord is in need of it." Your blessing is for God's glory, and your wealth is for the advancement of the kingdom of God. Jesus needs you. God further told the pharaoh through Moses to let His people go so that they may serve Him.

Your ultimate purpose is to worship God. Being free to enjoy life is to serve Him. Your freedom is for the glory of God, and you are alive to lift up the name of Jesus. For He said, "And when I am lifted up from the earth, I will draw everyone to myself" (John 12:32, NLT).

Remember: Jesus died for you; now it is your turn to live for Him. The Lord is in need of you.

Write Your Prayers and Thoughts Here

Afterword

This book should be used as an interactive tool to assist you in learning how to pray with anything and everything. At the end of each chapter, write some of your own prayers or write down your prayers with a date. Whenever the prayers are answered, write it in your book.

Teach your children and grandchildren how to pray casual but effective prayers. Teach them as they are putting away their toys that God will help them to put away any naughty behavior that they may have. As they are pulling out their toys, teach them to thank God for the many toys that they have.

We pray that this book will become one of your favorites. We pray that you will develop a more intimate relationship with your Lord and Savior, Jesus Christ.

If you have any questions or concerns about your spiritual walk with Christ, feel free to contact my wife and me (odoyin12@gmail.com). Please share this book with others and contact us concerning our copyright policy.

—Doctors Alexander and Angela Ikomoni

Our Biographies

Dr. Alexander and Dr. Angela Ikomoni are a "power couple" called to be a voice for the voiceless to empower the less privileged and destroy Satan's infrastructure: poverty. They are credentialed by the Pentecostal Theological Seminary in Cleveland, Tennessee, and have received their PhDs from the American Bible University and Aidan University, respectively. Together they founded BCI School of Chaplaincy and BCI School of Theology, where they serve as president and vice president. They are also founders and pastors of White Dove Church of God in Stockbridge, Georgia, USA.

They also authored the book called *Poverty Destroyed Forever* (forthcoming).

The Ikomonis are blessed with three wonderful children.

Printed in the USA
CPSIA information can be obtained
at www.ICGtesting.com
LVHW010438300923
759618LV00043B/926